T0274174

Black Women, Ivory Tower

Black Women, Ivory Tower

REVEALING THE LIES OF WHITE SUPREMACY IN AMERICAN EDUCATION

Jasmine L. Harris, PhD

Broadleaf Books

Minneapolis

BLACK WOMEN, IVORY TOWER
Revealing the Lies of White Supremacy in American Education

Copyright © 2024 Jasmine L. Harris. Published by Broadleaf Books, an imprint of 1517 Media. All rights reserved. Except for brief quotations in critical articles or reviews, no part of this book may be reproduced in any manner without prior written permission from the publisher. Email copyright@1517.media or write to Permissions, Broadleaf Books, PO Box 1209, Minneapolis, MN 55440-1209.

Library of Congress Cataloging-in-Publication Data

Names: Harris, Jasmine L., author.
Title: Black women, ivory tower : revealing the lies of white supremacy in American education / Jasmine L. Harris.
Description: Minneapolis : Broadleaf Books, 2023. | Includes bibliographical references.
Identifiers: LCCN 2023011786 (print) | LCCN 2023011787 (ebook) | ISBN 9781506489834 (hardback) | ISBN 9781506489841 (ebook)
Subjects: LCSH: Racism in higher education--United States. | Sexism in higher education--United States. | African American women in higher education. | African American women--Education (Higher)
Classification: LCC LC212.42 .H374 2023 (print) | LCC LC212.42 (ebook) | DDC 378.1/982996073--dc23/eng/20230426
LC record available at https://lccn.loc.gov/2023011786
LC ebook record available at https://lccn.loc.gov/2023011787

Cover design: Leah Jacobs Gordon

Print ISBN: 978-1-5064-8983-4
eBook ISBN: 978-1-5064-8984-1

Printed in China

For all the Davis women, the Fanning women, and the
Harris women—Black women who have lit my path. I see you.
This is for you.

Contents

1

A Meager Inheritance

"My grandma and great-grandma went to Vassar too," the blond, white girl added as she pointed out important landmarks on campus. We lived on the same floor, though only two days into college attendance, all that really meant was that we were strangers who shared a very unprivate bathroom and knew each other's names— though even that last part was dubious. I was the only Black person on the Jewett Hall tower floor, which was not unexpected at a school where the Black population hovers around 4 percent, but this was a new wrinkle. I naively assumed that at least all of us freshmen had an unfamiliarity with this place in common. I guess maybe I thought a few students would have a leg up because an older sibling or other *singular and distant* relative had attended Vassar College decades ago, but what I encountered was something else, a belonging I couldn't relate to, a relationship to this place that I could not replicate. That this girl traced her lineage back more than one hundred years at this school indicated her close relationship

1

to higher education. Her seemingly innocuous statement outlined a reproduction of intellectualism on which schools like this were founded, but I didn't know that yet. I was surrounded by "legacy" students with deep and perpetual ties to the institution. In fact, my class included the highest percentage of admitted legacy students to date in the school's history.[1] Policies that consider those deep familial bonds to the institution in admissions decisions fundamentally shift the demographics of college campuses at the country's most elite schools. Legacy students know the school's buildings, walkways, traditions, and at Vassar, even the trees—stars in their own right on a campus that doubles as a national arboretum. Legacy students are able to establish this place as theirs from the first day. I didn't have the same luxury.

When I arrived on Vassar's campus in 2001, I was the second person in my family to attend a school this prestigious—though I didn't yet know that, either. Not the second person to attend college, mind you. My grandmother, Leah, in the early 1940s, and great-grandmother, Alberta, in the late 1890s, attended Philander Smith College, a historically Black college in Little Rock, Arkansas. My mother attended the University of Wisconsin–Madison in the mid-1970s, and I have a handful of cousins with degrees from a variety of Historically Black Colleges and Universities (HBCUs), state universities, and community colleges across the country. But Vassar was different; it felt different, and my family regarded it as such. I was 1,200 miles away from home, among the ivy-laced buildings where American higher education was founded, in a place where a talkative middle-class Black girl from the Midwest inherently did not belong. It was also the place where, if I could succeed, I would expand what was possible for me in immeasurable ways.

Belonging in education, especially higher education, can't simply be manifested by desire or will. An individual's presence in school isn't indicative of their relationship to the place itself or their ability to integrate successfully. Instead, those things—belonging and connection— are bestowed upon people, mostly white, deemed appropriate in these "intellectual" spaces. Willpower and grit may improve achievement for Black people in school, but it doesn't guarantee our belonging. External effort doesn't translate to the intangible benefits of perceptions of belonging for us either. Our perseverance is evidence of the violent conditions in which we're educated, not an indication of inclusion in educational settings. School, because of its ability to expand one's networks and improve the chances of upward social mobility, is a persistent battleground for access to the place. Schools create and maintain race, gender, and class hierarchies in the United States. It is a place where we all need to belong, even if we cannot.

I come from a generation of women with college diplomas but with little intergenerational upward class mobility over the last one hundred years because, although the women before me accessed higher education, it didn't provide generational capital to pass down as it has for their white counterparts. That's what happens when entrance into education is given, but belonging is not. Their educational achievement is a triumph, but the lack of lasting benefits on their life chances are evidence of the superficial connections to education historically allowed to Black women.

Historically White-Serving Institutions

College attendance in Black communities remains low in comparison to white communities across time, in part because for Black people as a whole, education—especially higher education—is not a given, thanks to the continuing effects of a one hundred-year prohibition on educational access for Black communities. Our presence in college classrooms is not assumed, and belonging—however weak—must be wrested from the clutches of an institution founded in white supremacy and therefore unwilling, and in some ways, unable to provide it. Education as an American institution structures and restructures white supremacy in an eternal loop, formalizing the Black underclass by limiting the quality of education we can access and what can be extracted from education to improve our lives. For us, knowledge literally does not equal power.

This disassociation from education is done via a foundation of racialized inheritance on which the United States is built. College admissions, and therefore subsequent job opportunities, network access, and wealth accumulation, are one mechanism by which individuals have the opportunity to accumulate valuable educational capital, the tangible benefits of attending certain schools, achieving particular accolades in their lifetimes, and passing down that access to their children. But Black college graduates don't accumulate and pass down educational capital in the same ways as their white peers. This distinction in educational capital exists because the social value of education is less for Black graduates without the benefit of assumed belonging in higher education settings. When I walk into a room, no one assumes I am a Vassar graduate, even when I'm outfitted in Vassar-branded swag. I'm still more likely to be a visitor than a member of the Vassar community—both statistically *and* in public perception.

Most of the modern conceptions of higher education are built around the premise of universities as extended families, ignoring the positioning of Black graduates as inherently not a part of the college "family" at all. College degrees increase annual income and net worth, but for Black graduates, increases in income are small. Black students also account for less than 10 percent of all students at elite, historically white-serving institutions, schools with the highest degree value post-graduation, reifying issues of resource access in Black communities even as college graduation rates, especially among Black women, continue to increase.

Confining college admissions, and therefore subsequent job opportunities, network access, and wealth accumulation to white men, from the founding of Harvard University in 1636 and the College of William and Mary in 1693, has had lasting impacts on who among us are likely to accumulate valuable educational capital in their lifetimes, and then have the opportunity to pass down that access to their children. In 2022, income and wealth disparities persist as the overwhelming whiteness of higher education maintains disadvantages across social and economic landscapes for Black people.[2] With limited access to the country's most prestigious and predominantly white colleges and universities, Black college graduates acquire very little for their families to inherit.

Today Black college students make up, on average, 10 percent of college and university student populations,[3] more at HBCUs and less at prestigious predominantly white institutions. Each year, over a million degrees are conferred to white graduates, while less that 175,000 are conferred to Black students.[4] An essay in the college alumni magazine *Vassar Quarterly*, published in winter of my freshman year, quoted a white woman alumnus, whose daughter had just begun her freshman year, describing the college as her family's "ancestral home." The quote struck me because that's not a moniker available to Black families with similar lineage connections to higher education. Vassar's historical policies on the admission of Black students (the first was admitted in 1940) mean that I literally cannot have a generations-long connection to this school, specifically because of my race. I can be a graduate, an alumnus, but never ancestrally connected.

Building university campus culture around the concept of family, where university alumni status—and with it access to the social networks and intrinsic value imbued in the university name—makes belonging one of the most precious things to pass down and share with children and grandchildren. To do so ignores the racism-perpetuating narratives of family on college campuses where Black people, though present, were not then and are not now "family" at all. This organization of higher education ensures we're guests, outsiders to the institutional family—outnumbered and unwelcome. For this reason, historically white-serving schools will be called Historically White-Serving Colleges and Universities (HWSCUs) throughout this book to highlight the racialized foundations of higher education and to juxtapose them more adequately with HBCUs created to combat the policies of exclusion at HWSCUs across time.

In 2016, Black students comprised 9 percent of Ivy league freshman,[5] and today Black students are more underrepresented at elite HWSCUs than they were in 1980.[6] Connections to prestigious institutions, especially Ivy League schools, potentially improve an individual's social outcomes, either maintaining or improving class status and annual earnings across generations.[7] The ability to inherit prestigious educational access has ramifications well beyond the education itself. But little inheritable belonging is available for Black students, especially at prestigious institutions, so there was little belonging up for grabs for me as I navigated the structural and cultural landscape of Vassar's campus.

College "Inheritance"

Using race and gender identity first to prohibit and then to constrain college attendance perpetuates stagnant intergenerational mobility in Black communities, as evidenced by the short legacy of Black people in higher education. College degrees improve an individual's annual income by $17,500 on average,[8] but Black college graduates earn 20 percent less in annual income than white college graduates.[9] Black women in particular confront intersecting dominations of power constructed to limit access to higher education, especially at HWSCUs. When gender is also considered, Black women are penalized heavily, averaging less than seventy cents for every dollar earned by white college-educated men, seven cents less than white college-educated women.[10]

Attendance at prestigious colleges and universities improves these numbers, but Black women still fall way behind, and despite decades of affirmative action, Black attendance at the country's top colleges is perpetually low.[11] The stagnation of Black wealth accumulation since the 1970s indicates weak links between education and income even as Black students are being admitted to college in record numbers every year.[12] Those weak links are evidence of the unquantifiable value of belonging and educational capital in American society.

Black women degree holders, whose rate of college attendance has increased 72 percent since 1996,[13] are specifically limited in their ability to hold educational capital and pass down educational inheritance because the minority presence of Black students means weak institutional ties from their first days on campus. In 2022, even amid ever-increasing rates of Black women entering college, white women are still twice as likely to be there.

In an economy where the majority of salaried positions require advanced education, college degrees are a gatekeeping tool, preserving access to middle- and upper-class membership via those stable jobs. For example, Harvard University's class of 2021 included 29 percent legacy students.[14] One-third of the students admitted to the most prestigious school in the country in 2018 were there in part because of their ancestors' attendance. The majority of these students are white and wealthy, and their admittance is a reflection of preserved racial hierarchies in American education. Education is one system that's mostly gone unchecked in the structural perpetuation of white wealth over time. As college degrees become increasingly vital to potential wealth accumulation, affiliation with prestigious HWSCUs is even more significant than in previous decades. Educational inheritance then provides the social power to bestow intangible inheritance to static institutions and is more valuable than personal property, money, or rights.

Limiting access to prestigious HWSCUs also serves to maintain the social narrative of Black people as disinterested in or unable to intellectually grasp advanced education. Low rates of Black matriculation became, as a result, the expectation rather than the rule, stunting generations of educational inheritance for Black students while white students benefited from the increasingly important capital derived from an elite education. On the frontlines of American desegregation, Black women bore the brunt of tactics meant to scare them back to segregated schools, but increased high school graduation rates for Black women didn't spill over to increase college acceptance rates until the early twenty-first century.

Ambitious

"This is an ambitious list," the white male guidance counselor I'd been assigned began. I was still new at this suburban Michigan school, but a quick analysis of my surroundings signaled it was less prestigious and more diverse than the school from which I'd transferred in Apple Valley, Minnesota. This man's clear combination of overwork and disinterest suggested I'd have an even harder time here than in Minnesota. We moved to follow my mom's dreams up the corporate ladder, and I (rightfully) worried about how I'd fit in to the classroom here. This man had not read my transcripts closely, nor was he willing to take an interest in a new Black girl—even one who'd been in the top twenty-five in her previous high school class (not that he was aware of that).

I was one of hundreds of students my counselor was required to counsel throughout the college admissions process, and it was probably easier to surmise my prospects based on my race and gender, rather than evaluating my ability. His response was not unexpected but especially aggravating given my academic standing—let's just say it was high. I sighed, "Is it?" My list, fifteen schools in all, included a handful of schools in California and Hawaii to fulfill my dreams of living in a warm-weather climate, Vassar College (my eventual choice) and a few other Seven Sisters colleges to appease my mom's desire to see me at a small school with close proximity to professors, the requisite Ivy League schools—just in case—and lastly, a few Midwestern state schools whose only purpose was to prevent conversations like this one. Yet here we were anyway, staring at one another askance.

I'll describe my mother's immediate and no-nonsense response after she learned about this meeting in later chapters, but my guidance counselor took a relatively hands-off approach after their interaction. And honestly, that probably felt for him like the only alternative to actually helping me through the process. It never occurred to him that I might be qualified to attend the schools on my list. There are so few narratives, even at the turn of the twenty-first century, that he'd never just assume my academic success. Without that assumption, why would he voluntarily take a second look at my file?

The lack of historical narratives of Black college students positions us as anomalies—not evidence of Black achievement, but a result of the law of averages. We were there based on luck (and perhaps affirmative action) more than anything else. Black students don't just gain higher education membership through attendance the way property owners buy membership to the "right" neighborhoods (close to modern conveniences, with good schools and safe public areas). We have to prove we deserve to have even been given access to the same spaces where white people's deservedness is preordained by race. Then, we have to *earn* belonging. Being a student at a prestigious institution isn't the same as belonging there. I wanted to belong at Vassar, even if I was broke compared to my friends, despite being sexually assaulted, and regardless of the limited available support network. I willingly left myself open to unending terror attempting to be a Vassar girl, unaware of the darkness of white supremacy in a place like that and the violence I'd be required to endure to stay.

Belonging, especially in higher education, is rooted in this system of inheritance, capital conversion, and additional value accumulation. The system primarily benefits white men because they are (1) more likely than other groups to inherit something, (2) more likely to assume legal possession of their inheritance, and (3) more likely to convert their inheritance value into even more prestige.[15] College education and its system of legacy admissions is one mechanism by which inheritance and capital are intertwined. Stunted admission of Black students is another, and the last and perhaps most insidious is decreasing Black faculty hires at HWSCUs. Black women like me are least likely to benefit from educational belonging because of the unlikelihood that I inherit anything of value or because, should I actually come into inheritance, the benefits accompanying that inheritance are never publicly assumed.

The connections between education, inheritance, and capital are racially constructed and defined via admissions guidelines, legacy, and hiring policies that outline belonging in educational spaces. As a result, perceived non-belonging among Black students on college campuses is high, increasing with the racial disparity of the campus population.[16] Once there, mental and physical fatigue makes degree completion difficult. And after graduation, for the less than 10 percent of Black students who graduate from these schools, the value of their alumni status—and therefore the value of that status to their children—is less than that of whites graduating from the same school.

A History of Non-Belonging

Restricting the education of enslaved people was a method of domination used to block the potential for social, economic, or psychological freedom, and as a useful, but perhaps unintended consequence, prevented the use of educational inheritance afforded to white graduates for centuries. Forcibly brought to the United States, enslaved, then strategically blocked from the social and economic benefits of formal education around which modern class status would be structured, the threads between race, gender, and educational capital are woven via the American slave codes, including laws prohibiting their education. These laws, government sanctioned and socially constructed, provided the foundation for a century of educational lag in Black communities, a sense of non-belonging in educational institutions, and an inability to inherit or pass down educational capital.

The myth of education as the great equalizer was the basis of desegregation advocacy in the 1950s and at the center of the Supreme Court decision in *Brown v. Board of Education*.[17] By the time of the case's 1954 decision, it was already clear that access to quality education was an important ingredient in the recipe for upward social mobility, and lack of access was devastating for Black people who, by 1965 comprised 10 percent of the population but held less than

2 percent of the wealth in the United States.[18] The deep wealth disparity is in part a result of a post-emancipation century of minimal structural supports aimed at improving Black American lives. Meanwhile, the white people around them were being provided institutional support to jumpstart legacies of wealth and prosperity,[19] especially via higher education. President Roosevelt's 1944 GI Bill sent hundreds of thousands of World War II veterans to college, but by 1946 only five thousand Black veterans were registered students. Black GIs around the country shared similar experiences of seeking higher education with full funding and being turned away at the door.[20] Instead, the Black applicants blocked from these schools often attended one of the then 121 HBCUs, founded by states to fulfill the second Morrill Act of 1890 requiring states to establish a separate land-grant college for Black students if they were excluded from the existing land-grant college because of their race.[21]

Stripping college degree attainment for Black graduates of the same value afforded white graduates continues to racialize derivable educational capital. There are countless stories of Black doctors, lawyers, judges, and professors presumed incompetent in public and professional settings despite their degree credentials. I've had students explicitly question my qualification to teach them based solely on my appearance. For Black people, because assumptions of low academic success are mapped onto our skin by longstanding social narratives about our capabilities, it's less about what we've accomplished and more about what we look like. We must scream our achievements from the mountaintops, or else they are ignored, rendered invisible and unknowable because they are inconceivable in the ways society has prewritten our stories. This is a practical example of racism making race look biological.

On the institutional side, HBCUs have suffered from weaker educational capital caused by a century of undervaluing attendance at segregated schools.[22] Those designated HBCUs did the heavy lifting of educating Black people for more than one hundred years. My family tree is filled with college degrees from HBCUs, but the carry-over is weak compared to the potential social and economic benefits of passing down that attendance. My hallmate's centuries-long connection to Vassar College, by contrast, includes a lifetime of potential payoff. These things work together to encourage internalized feelings of non-belonging in higher education, leaving Black students blaming themselves for difficulty achieving the same upward social mobility of their white peers rather than questioning the construction and function of education as an institution. Publicly discussed assumptions of incompetence and a devaluing of majority Black institutions are both meant to reify feelings of non-belonging post-graduation.

In 2022, Black students continue to document experiences of racism and discrimination at HWSCUs, both at the hands of individual students and the institutions' administrations. *Brown v. Board of Education* was meant to be a turning point in the social disadvantages of disparate access to quality education, but race-based hardships persist. When I responded, in that same meeting, to my high school guidance counselor's suggestion that my list of potential schools was too "ambitious" with, "Have you read my transcript?" I was immediately labeled as aggressive and combative rather than self-assured. "Miss Harris, I have no doubt you're a good student," he promised, while clearly doubting that very thing. "I just want you to have options. You'd hate to miss out on perfectly fine schools because you were shooting for the stars." Because striving for excellence is a recipe for disappointment for me, a Black girl, as his response implies. Apparently, I wasn't aiming low enough.

This is not particularly surprising given that education, at its inception, was created for the betterment of white men. More than that, though, higher education is a symbol of class status to which Black people rarely have access. Education, especially at prestigious HWSCUs, maintains a dangerous insistence on the ideology of Black communities as too innately unintelligent, lazy, or incapable of achieving any real social and economic success, altering the amount and types of educational capital that can be extracted and potentially passed down as a result. They (HWSCUs) may have to let some of us in, but they don't have to regard us as equals.

Once on campus, Black women in particular are structured as enemies to the systemic white supremacy of higher education— unqualified, untrustworthy, and unwelcome. Misogynoir, unique oppression at the intersections of racism and sexism reserved for Black women,[23] exposes us to experiences of discrimination in higher education meant to perpetuate feelings of non-belonging and to prevent the kind of student engagement that expands the value of our education. Even as universities admit more Black students, there is a continuing fear among white administrators, faculty, students, parents, and politicians of a surfeit of Black students "blackening" traditional white campus spaces and traditions. Preventing Black women students on campus from active participation in the campus community is not just demoralizing, and not only a question of access, it perpetuates the erasure of our stories.

This book examines the historic and continued process of structural and cultural quarantine of Black people from all facets of school, not just an increase in Black students' uncertainty about belongingness in school, but also the limited imagery of Black people across educational culture. It is a concerted effort to cement a concrete incompatibility between Black college students and the culture of higher education. At HWSCUs, like the one I attended, the white supremacist foundations mean that processes of integration are weak for Black students, but institutional regulation via campus social norms and explicit campus policies is high, creating an environment that discourages retention of Black students. We do not arrive on campus with the internalized feelings of belonging among our white peers. Colleges are racialized institutions,[24] because they legitimate the unequal distribution of resources by race and gender, diminish the agency of Black students, perpetuate weak credentialing for Black graduates, and execute institutional policies along racial lines. As such, the educational capital derived from college attendance is also racialized. What is left, then, for Black degree-holders to pass on?

What We Inherit

The unique orientation of Black people to higher education limits the usefulness of the concept of inheritance for Black college alumni. Legacy policies are one mechanism by which whiteness in higher education is perpetuated.[25] In the example of Harvard, to admit one-third of an entire class with legacy status means attendance at Harvard is inheritable. White parents and grandparents who attended the university when it was illegal for Black people to do so can pass down that opportunity to their white family members unencumbered. Those family members are then afforded the opportunity to accumulate additional social and economic capital as a result of their attendance and perpetuate already disproportionate income and wealth accumulation along racial lines. A system that, by design, Black people cannot infiltrate.

As evidence of the impact of educational capital, and by extension, inheritance, Harvard graduates report median family household incomes triple the national average, and are more employable than non-Harvard graduates, even in economic downturns. Their ability to invoke the Harvard name in job interviews, at networking events, and on professional social media sites makes attendance there invaluable.[26] Willful ignorance of the historical contexts under which relationships with United States colleges and universities were originally derived racializes educational inheritance and leaves little chance for Black people to gain similar access.

Minimizing the presence of Black students in higher education limits available narratives of Black success in college. Even my own family members have lost the direct connections to education and knowledge acquisition that could change feelings of non-belonging. My maternal great-grandmother, grandmother, and mother were college graduates—yes—but we, their descendants, did not inherit the same educational capital from their attendance as would white descendants. Each of these women graduated college despite the structural and cultural barriers to their academic success, not because of a profusion of support and alumni association after the fact. Their diplomas, however, did not ensure continued middle-class status for their descendants. Black people are increasingly more educated, but rather than being enculturated into higher education at a young age, the continuous erasure of Black successes in higher education perpetuates the inability to accumulate and pass on associated educational capital.

Such anecdotal assertions are not meant to essentialize my experiences as normal, instead serving as evidence of a pattern of educational inheritance structured around race. Black people are made to feel like they don't belong in school, whether they enjoy learning or not, because it isn't just about who's not in school; it's about making sure those who are there understand their place. I come from three generations of Black female college graduates, but I never had the opportunity to assert those connections. I had no stories to anchor my desire for learning to a legacy of Black educational achievement, no historical connection to bind me to these learning spaces. I did not and could not inherit and make tangible the social and economic benefits of their college attendance. I had to earn it all over again, from scratch, because the value of my intellect and hard work, and the intellect and hard work of this line of Black women kin, exist in generationally separated vacuums. One has very little impact on the others.

It's not just higher education attendance that can't be passed on. Very few academic successes can be held, publicly acknowledged, and passed down by Black people because we're unexpected and unwanted in academic spaces. Low rates of Black students in advanced placement courses,[27] college honors programs,[28] and with high standardized test scores highlights an inability to progress, but associated statistics are alternatively read as a difference in hard work and intellect between Black and white students.[29] The academic erasure of Black people has imposed violence on entire communities since the beginnings of formal education, and the civil inattention to Blackness on campus, the process that acknowledges Black students but never fully engages them as members of the campus culture, takes its toll in a multitude of ways. Acceptance of the naturalized whiteness of college diminishes the ability of Black people to integrate into higher education successfully. Likewise, hundreds of years of perpetuating Black people as uneducated and uneducable continues to socially and economically depress Black communities.

Black graduates of HWSCUs do still pass down alternative forms of educational capital to descendants. Instead of gaining full access to the institutional prestige of HWSCUs, Black graduates' status as college degree–holders is never assumed, even as their presence in higher education tracks continuously upward. Instead, Black graduates pass down the art of pretending to belong in higher education and the tools to help extend that performance beyond graduation to maintain institutional connections. Often what we share and pass down to one another are survival mechanisms, expectation setting, and access to racialized support systems. We gravitate toward each other at HWSCUs because our racial identity impacts everything that happens to us. Hence, respite is often only found in the formal (and informal) Black spaces we manage to carve out.

For Black college students, the most important form of educational capital is student-to-student. The spaces then become the things we pass down, not to our genetic family, but to the next generation of Black students to join the campus community. This isn't true of every HWSCU community, but those with a steady enrollment of Black students are likely to have identified spaces on campus where Black students feel safe. The protection of these boundaries, along with explanations of potential advocates, racial adversaries, and general patterns of cultural racism on campus is immediate and invaluable, access to which can drastically improve the experiences of Black students on campus and contribute to their academic success. It is inheritable educational capital. This book was written in that tradition. A place to capture stories of Black students' survival in predominantly white classrooms, reckoning with what's required for success in these often-violent environments.

This system is not fair, of course. Black students inherit educational capital that has a high value in the present but can rarely be used to accumulate additional capital after graduation. It doesn't improve our class status or likelihood of upward social mobility more than the degree itself. Even Black legacy students are less likely to be admitted to their parents' or grandparents' alma maters than white legacy students. Stories of three and four generations of Black family members at HBCUs are the exceptions rather than the rule.[30] Educational inheritance, then, will perhaps never exist for Black people in the same way as whites. Our non-belonging is too ingrained in the institution itself to provide space for beneficial connections and access to similar rates of upward social mobility for Black graduates. In this way, inheritance is racist; and racism is both cultural and incorporated into the structure and practice of higher education membership.

This book, and the stories within its pages, details the utter banality of my experiences against a backdrop of white supremacy and privilege at school as I attempted my own accumulation of educational inheritance. The meager inheritance afforded Black people by education, even as it becomes the main mechanism for upward social mobility and status for white people, isn't slowing down our entrance into higher education. But increasing numbers in college doesn't guarantee our safety there. The threads between past and present together tell us a story of suppressed belonging, but also perseverance. It shouldn't be this way, but it is. I wish someone had said that to me twenty-five years ago, so this is me, saying it to you. I've never, as a student, alumnus, or faculty member, felt like an extension of the HWSCUs with which I'm affiliated. Instead, I— like so many Black people traversing higher education—questioned what it is about my identity that means perpetual non-belonging. I'm not a member of these cultures, I am a critic.

2

The Power of a Story

"I'll try to remember what I can, but I'm not sure how much I know," my auntie Carolyn began as I prepped my recorder to capture the stories of relatives I never met or barely remember. In a family of chatty Black women, we're good for hours of talking about this and that, but we rarely share stories of the past, especially about school—and definitely not our experiences or expectations of treatment in those spaces. I'd reached out to the eldest of my mother's eight siblings to tell me everything she remembers about her mother and grandmother because I wanted to uncover their stories. Though I'd heard in passing that my grandmother and great-grandmother were college educated, it wasn't mentioned often, even my mother was vague on the details. I kept coming back to *why*. Why, if these Black women accomplished something as improbable as completing a college degree, would we not shout it from the rooftops, retelling and reliving their achievement, at least with each other, in perpetuity?

So I started out on this quest for information. Maybe I exist in the wake of a long history of educated Black women, women who demanded to be educated and commanded respect in return. Then, perhaps I could manifest belonging on college campuses in a way I hadn't before. But because their educations were reduced to rumors, I didn't know, and more than that, I wasn't exactly sure why I didn't know. To have braved what I imagine were inhumane living situations for Black people before the Civil Rights Movement, and not only have entered college, but completed degrees should be something we should brag about, right? Instead, at least in my family, their experiences in higher education existed obtusely, were rarely discussed, and made an imperceptible impact on our daily lives. My family is not unique. Very few stories are told across history about the triumphs of Black people in higher education, in part because we're still just now hitting precedent-setting milestones in this arena. When promoted to associate professor, I was the first Black woman to do so in my department ever. Never in the college's 150-year history had a Black woman in my discipline been promoted to a position that white men achieve yearly. There are no positive stories of the Black women who had this job before me, only acknowledgment of discontent. The only stories Black people really get to tell, especially in historically white-serving learning spaces, are of the indignities we're forced to suffer, the things we've overcome or managed to endure. This book is a testament to that. So, we hold tight to those stories we tell for each other to protect and uplift us

The education of Black women has always been political, rooted in white fears that we seek education for some inscrutable aim and with heavy economic and social consequences in our lives. Historically low levels of Black educational achievement are not a biological phenomenon then, but an institutional one—the lasting vestiges of the original Black slave codes banning our freedom to learn to read and write in an attempt to block our potential uprising. Restricting the education of slaves was a method of domination used to block the potential for social, economic, or psychological freedom. To maintain Black subordination post-Emancipation, public education in Black communities was degraded, preventing its use for the upward social mobility and educational capital provided to white graduates via the same institutions. Founded on this legacy of white supremacy, the policies and practices of education are written and rewritten to perpetuate a culture of *dis*-education in Black communities. Not simply limiting our access to education, but a disassociation from it, using language that implicates Black children in the destruction of their own communities, assumes they are uninterested in learning, and punishes their misdeeds more harshly and routinely than white children. A part of this process of diseducation includes removing our stories from the narrative history of Black achievement. It's not by accident or coincidence that my ancestors' college degrees exist only vaguely in my own family history. The continuous erasure of our narratives perpetuates the idea that we don't belong in educational spaces and that we don't deserve to be educated.

I grew up innately drawn toward learning spaces, but I've never felt at home in them. The personal, intimate feeling of belonging so many white students take for granted was unavailable to me from the start. Before I had the appropriate language to describe my discomfort in the classroom, I felt unwelcome there. Even now, the unease with which I must traverse educational spaces is palpable. I love learning, teaching, and generally spending time in places where people learn, but I've never been afforded belonging. I want education, but education doesn't want me. Even as I've uncovered deep and impressive educated Black women in my family tree, I still don't belong, just as they did not.

An Unexplained Attraction

From the moment I learned to read, I consumed any and everything, averaged A's, and even taught myself algebra in the tenth grade when I had the unfortunate draw of the wrestling coach for a teacher. But I also constantly found myself in detention (and one in-school suspension) for seemingly minor infractions relative to my peers, and often my teachers commented that I was "too chatty" and "distracted" other students. My participation felt unwanted in the classroom, and my achievements were treated as an annoyance. I wrestled with the dissonance between my hunger for information and my distaste for the day-to-day experience of being in that space without anyone to validate my confusion. I hadn't yet heard the stories of my great-aunt's time at Columbia University's Teachers College pursuing a master's degree in Harlem, New York, at the tail end of the Harlem Renaissance, or learned that my grandmother and almost all ov her attended college in the Jim Crow–era South.

So I felt oddly drawn to learning new things but couldn't explain the attraction. At home, the importance of good grades was stressed, but my family showed little excitement about my learning. For me, learning felt like absorbing and expanding; it was a purely exhilarating feeling at first. I still remember the first time that learning felt both fun and isolating. I was eleven-and-a-half years old and we were dissecting owl pellets, those small globs of their regurgitated meals, in my middle school science class. I picked through the tangled mass as delicately as my fat sixth-grade fingers wielding small tweezers could. I felt scientific and, for the first time, really understood what that meant. The happy trance of such delicate work engaged my scientific thinking and active learning for the first time. The methodical process of freeing each small bone from the hair and the unidentifiable owl vomit surrounding it led me to question all sorts of things I'd never previously considered. My brain started working beyond just what animal the owl had consumed (the assignment) to all manner of more complex existential questions (not the assignment). In fact, to this day, I am extremely fascinated by birds (unlike my sister who is terrified of them), imaging myself as a novice bird watcher and enthusiast, interests that began on that day examining owl pellets.

The ensuing class discussion was to be my masterpiece, suddenly invigorated by school work rather than the independent projects I came up with at home. I couldn't wait to seriously engage with my fellow students and my teacher via questions and comments about our archaeological discoveries. I can't remember exactly what I said when finally called upon—something about how humans ate versus how owls ate, but I remember the silence afterward. The uncomfortable feeling as no one responded. I could almost feel the discontent of my classmates and teacher around my additions to the afternoon's lecture, and that feeling was instantly embedded in memories and often recalled as a warning about my position in predominantly white classrooms. The stark message of my non-belonging was conveyed at that moment. Then, after a long beat, the teacher called on someone else, leaving my comment hanging— utterly ignored—in front of me, a signal not to call on me again.

The bond I thought I shared with my white peers was broken by their silence. No one came to my defense, as we often did when feelings of unfairness surfaced in interactions between student and teacher. I was truly alone in that moment and in that space. I slunk down into my chair under the weight of that loneliness, under the realization that there would be no defense of my comments because, coming from me, they were indefensible. Not wrong or bad. But not defendable because they came from a know-it-all Black girl in a class filled with white faces. I could be as inquisitive as I pleased, but my thoughts and ideas would rarely be acceptable in academic settings. There was no empathetic connection between me, teacher, and students. My outsider status was marked with the proverbial scarlet letter *B* for Black girl. It wasn't until much later when I'd become a professional academic that I'd meet Black students who'd grown up in predominantly Black classrooms with Black teachers without the same traumatic memories. Instead, theirs are memories of support and engagement meant to encourage continued intellectual exploration as opposed to having those impulses squashed as often happened to me.

Such anecdotal assertions are not meant to essentialize my experiences as normal. In fact, it wasn't until my doctoral work that I'd read enough to begin piecing together the what, how, and why of my experiences at school. At last, I had enough information to realize I wasn't *abnormal.* I had language to discuss my grievances, so mine can't possibly be a single story but rather evidence of historical patterns. Later, as my research trajectory zoomed in on educational experiences in Black communities, I came to understand what happened to me as standard. Across two centuries, Black women have been segregated by the spatial, social, and temporal facets of the United States school system, subjected to unrelenting scrutiny and invasive surveillance. Our stories, mine included, are bound together in the activist history of educational freedom—field notes revealing the culture of Black diseducation, the structural and cultural quarantine of Black people from all facets of school, and the details of its construction. But why did it take so long for me to learn that many of my experiences were structurally created rather than internally formed?

Our academic erasure has imposed symbolic violence—that acceptance of naturalized social deficits created by white supremacist structures—on Black people for three centuries. Negatively impacting our ability to be successfully integrated into school and encouraging us to blame ourselves for those failures. In reality, tracking systems, hyper-discipline, and a lack of exposure to Black culture among nearly all white teaching and administrative staff work together to encourage a distrust of or disinterest in school among Black kids. It only took a few generations of popular culture portraying Black people as uneducated and uneducable to embed this ideology within Black communities; its members are unable to distinguish whether the idea was placed within our collective consciousness by outside forces or had biological origins. This system of Black diseducation simultaneously maintains and is maintained by Black economic suppression. The assumption of Black non-belonging in higher education is internalized in my family such that our history of academic achievement is rarely discussed with any fanfare. It is as though a family of Black siblings attending college in 1930s Arkansas, like mine, was perfunctory rather than exceptional; not ordinary, as in it's no big deal because everyone does it, but worse than that—forgotten, in the face of more pressing issues of survival.

Black people are made to feel like they don't belong in school, whether they enjoy learning or not. If Black diseducation is about maintaining racial hierarchies, then school is one of the first places where Black students learn the social disdain of Blackness. So, even when we do succeed, the stories feel untellable. And it almost worked on me. I almost fully internalized the idea that school just wasn't *for me*. I had no stories to anchor my desire for learning to a legacy of Black educational achievement and, I thought, no historical connection to bind me to these learning spaces. What I wanted, what I still want, is to belong in spaces designed specifically to keep me out—to belong at school.

What I didn't know are stories of a long line of Black women before me, the most radical among us who've always sought out information and learning regardless of the consequences. Black women have a history of forcing our education where we're unwanted, not out of some innate grit, but out of survival. Our arrival in academe—was and still is—met with hostility. Our fight to remain is constant because our continued relegation to the margins is something worth rebelling against, and our education is too socially valuable to give up. The stories of Black women who fought the hardest, most dangerous battles for acceptance in academia have been methodically erased from public discourse. Even in my own family, long legacies of education are just now being uncovered, lost in generations of other, more immediate, struggles. I, unfortunately, can only imagine the power of repeating these stories for generations of Black girls facing down the unwelcome classroom and the potentially positive impact on my own general well-being on this path. This disassociation of Black people from education is a form of political terrorism. Even with familial retellings, the power of such stories, especially for othered groups like Black women, exists just beyond our reach. They are there, but lost to time, familial obligations, and disinterest. So who does have access to them? If stories about Black academic achievement are not accessible to Black students, their impact on Black students' continued success is minimal. This book tries to amplify those stories and, with them, a long history of Black educational belonging.

Education is political because information is imbued with power, a potential weapon against the intersecting powers that maintain our second class citizenship in the United States. Learning, first reading and writing, then critical thinking and discourse skills, makes Black people dangerous and less susceptible to the symbolic, if not physical, violence of white supremacy. Collective recognition of our potential for high achievement shifts the narrative of what it means to be a Black student. Sharing our stories, not just mine but those of so many Black women before me, creates a pattern of educational experiences woven across time and space, connecting us in a collection of data undeniably asserting our belonging in the hallowed ivory halls of the academic tower. These are some of those stories.

College Girls

I felt like an outsider from my first day at Vassar College, the ivy-covered Hudson Valley liberal arts school so famous for producing haughtily educated white women groomed for upper-class living that the phrase "Vassar girl" is strewn across pop culture from *Some Like it Hot* to *The Simpsons*.[1] I knew none of the college's history at the time, having chosen the school last minute on the urging of my mother who'd heard stories of the elite education I'd receive. She was convinced that what I needed to reinvigorate my thirst for learning was the freedom I'd come to perceive as unavailable in public school education, and Vassar, with its small classes and prestigious professors, promised to deliver me after four years, a highly educated and independent thinker.

It turns out those "stories she heard" about Vassar were closer to home than my mother let on at the time. "I remember when you were applying to colleges, and I told your mother Vassar was the place for you," my godmother, Sharon, mentioned to me casually during a late night catch-up with her and my mother on a fall 2022 visit home to Minnesota. "*You* were the friend who told her about Vassar?" I asked incredulously because this was no small revelation. At thirty-nine years old, exactly how I ended up at Vassar twenty-one years earlier was still of a bit of a mystery to me. "Oh yeah, it was Sharon. I guess I never told you that," Mom interjected. "Because I went to Wellesley," Sharon added. "A Seven Sisters school," Sharon and I said almost simultaneously. Then, like we'd both learned long ago at our respective schools, we tried to name all the others—the perfect test for a Vassar girl still trying to belong.

All of this was new information for me. I'd always assumed Sharon and my mom met in college at Madison because she, like my mother, grew up in Milwaukee. But they actually met in flight attendant school. So this woman—my mother's best friend, a woman with whom I've spent a fair amount of my life for someone who is not a blood relation, the woman who took me to my driver's license test at sixteen years old and let me use her car for the exam—had such a colossal impact on my decision of where to attend college and I had no idea. I had no idea about her educational accomplishments, no idea of this connection to Vassar, however minimal, that would've helped me feel a sense of belonging there. I wasn't a legacy per se, but I was close enough in the canon that I might've been able to feign an institutional connection. Another story gone untold until too late.

My mother and godmother were mostly right in their belief that Vassar would be important for me. It was here where I first learned true analysis, but the development of that skill also meant that I began to understand my role as the other, to feel the effects of a history of our displacement from the very institution I was now attending. When Black people were outright prevented from higher education, many who could pass as white did so to gain access; others depended on white allies for support and recommendation. But more often than not we were still turned away, portrayed as less capable, then—in a strategic pivot—labeled political villains and denied high wages upon graduation, should we succeed. Across history, Black women have demanded education and been punished for their audacity to do so. I felt that tension just as much at Vassar as anywhere else. I arrived without the knowledge of my family's

Ivy League pedigree, or the number of college degrees preceding me. Those are the stories, like my hallmate who can trace her lineage to the college's early years, that make students perceive belonging in these "hallowed" spaces—and I had none.

Being a Black "college girl" was *always* an oxymoron. In 1860, five years before slavery would be federally illegal, Rebecca Lee Crumpler, a Black freewoman from Delaware, entered New England Female Medical School. Accepted on the recommendation of the doctor whom she worked under as a nurse for many years, Dr. Crumpler was an unusual sight in such a space, especially when just attending college was unlikely for a Black woman. To see her in medical school, where even Black men were rarely admitted, was improbable. Expectedly, her presence was not well-received by the all-white faculty who labeled her a slow thinker and were hesitant to pass her. Dr. Crumpler's focus on homeopathic training, a then emerging field of medical study, was villainized. But in 1864, Dr. Crumpler became the first Black woman to earn a doctorate of medicine.[2] Even before the majority of Black people in this country had their freedom, Dr. Crumpler pushed for freedom of education. She forced her way through medical school on undeniable talent so compelling that the doctors under whom she learned in medical school advocated for her graduation when the board hesitated to award her doctorate.[3]

After medical school, Dr. Crumpler focused on providing healthcare for women and children in Boston, opening a practice with her husband. She'd later write *Book of Medical Discourses* specifically for an audience of women interested in information about how to care for the health of their own families, and potentially without access to formal medicine.[4]

Understanding the value of her acquired knowledge, Dr. Crumpler breached the impermeable world of medical information and passed it on to those without the same access. She brought the information back to the area where she spent her formative years and wrote in a style accessible to the audience for which it was most useful. She used her education to educate others and begin a legacy of educational uplift among Black women, even when doing so seemed impossible. Dr. Crumpler's impact on education advocacy for Black women is all but erased from history books, just one example among countless others in which Black women are punished for bringing information back to their communities. Her plain writing style made her an outcast in the social networks of many local white doctors, and she was never published in medical journals.[5] Dr. Crumpler's narrative, rooted in a deep understanding of the value of higher education, highlights a singular triumph over racism and white supremacy, but is noticeably absent from common historical retellings, lessening the social weight of her achievements.

That Dr. Crumpler graduated medical school pre-emancipation is an extraordinary feat, and an unusual story for the time. Few Black women were allowed entrance into college or graduate school before the 1940s. Instead, they attended segregated HBCUs,[6] or (if they were able) attempted to pass as white—a much more dangerous proposition. At my own alma mater, its first Black student, Anita Hemmings, passed as white until her race was revealed shortly before graduation. Hemmings graduated in 1897 as the first Black woman to do so at Vassar College and one of very few to do so at schools of Vassar's reputation. As a presumed descendant of Sally Hemmings and Thomas Jefferson, Anita Hemmings grew up battling racism and being tempted by the overwhelming possibility of passing as white. Making the choice to pass as white to circumvent the immovable barriers to education posed by her Blackness meant she had to split her consciousness in two, shunning her family, performing whiteness nonstop, and turning away from cultural membership in the Black community, fractured.[7]

Hemmings's story is often retold, especially in Vassar lore, as the first hints at the school's present culture of "progressiveness." But Hemmings's graduation was not acknowledged as a sign of changing times. Instead, it became a national scandal with her "dark beauty" blamed for masking her racial deceit, her purported charm and affability, weapons in her theft of a degree otherwise off limits to her. Newspapers from Albany to Philadelphia questioned what it might mean to allow this Black woman to graduate college and what other ideas Black people might get in the wake of her success. These questions were asked, and her story was told, not as an encouragement to other Black people interested in attending segregated schools but as a warning to white people that closer attention must be paid to the white supremacist gatekeeping process in higher education.

Held as one of the most beautiful, talented, and charming students in her class, Hemmings spent three-and-a-half years playing the part of classic white Vassar girl, whose olive complexion exoticized her as perhaps of Native American descent and only encouraged faint whispers that she may be something, and someone, unwelcome. Her identity as Black was only revealed after Hemmings's roommate, Louise "Lulu" Taylor, suspicious of her true racial background and jealous of her popularity—especially among the Yale men—alerted her father. Lulu's father, in turn, hired a private investigator to track down Hemmings's family, uncovering her true racial identity. Hemmings's parents, both mulattos living in the mostly Black Roxbury neighborhood in Boston, had conspired with their daughter to send her to Vassar as a white woman, listing her ancestry as French and English. The choice wasn't an unusual one at the time, regardless of its danger. It would be a full forty years before Vassar College would willingly admit Black women. Dr. June (Jackson) Christmas would graduate from Vassar as one of the first publicly identified Black woman in 1944, forty-seven years after Hemmings.

Dr. Christmas received the 2003 Award for Distinguished Alumni Achievement from Vassar in the winter of my sophomore year, another acknowledgment of the almost outlandishness of my own place there. Before me, in the Aula—the oft-meeting space for identity-centric events on campus—was this woman, Dr. Christmas, who was the same age as my grandmother and one of the first Black women graduates from the school. During my early years at Vassar, I was educated among white women whose lineage could be traced through the Vassar halls for generations, with connections to women long dead. In contrast, this woman, one of the first openly Black woman to successfully survive this place, was standing before me.

The recency of our inclusion hit me hard, intensified my resolve to overachieve on campus, and simultaneously shocked my psyche into a dark hole of uncertainty. The kind of double-consciousness I experienced then, as I increasingly struggled with my understanding of self in this space, was not unlike W.E.B. Du Bois's early theorizing but specific to this place of education,[8] a nebulous feeling of resignation over my necessity in the institution, but an acknowledgment that I'd never truly be allowed to belong in the tradition of knowledge gathering. Here, I realized I could be a Black student but never truly a Vassar girl.

At the time, it felt like I'd been doomed to perpetually strive for some unreachable threshold for success, a point that I dared myself to reach by out-accomplishing everyone around me. I spread myself thin with acapella, rugby, administrative boards, and student leadership positions. I rarely slept, hardly ate, became an active cutter, self-medicated, and slipped into undiagnosed depression trying to make my achievements on campus seem effortless—to be a true Vassar girl. And I was heartbroken by the realization that would never happen. Hemmings, too, was heartbroken after her revelation as a Black woman derailed her previous accomplishments. Being outed stripped her of the moniker of "Vassar girl" and all of the social capital with which it is imbued—just as she hoped it could be hers.

But Hemmings didn't give up. After marrying a Black man capable of and interested in passing himself, the pair raised their three children as white. In 1923, thirty years later, she enrolled her daughter, Ellen Love, in school at Vassar as a white woman, determined that she would become the true Vassar girl Hemmings was denied embodying.[9] Again, it was Hemmings's roommate, still bitter over the indecency of rooming with a Negro unknowingly all those years ago, who alerted Vassar administrators to Hemmings's repeat offense. And again, the college was indecisive in its decision-making but allowed Love to graduate in 1927 as a white woman—a Vassar girl.

All three of these women, Dr. Crumpler, Anita Hemmings, and her daughter Ellen Love, circumvented the color line standing between them and the higher education that teased a better future with the tools they had. Their stories reflect the constant conflict of race and education for Black women anxious to cement their place within the institution, and the hostility—tepid hostility at best, open hostility at worst—with which we are met upon arrival in predominantly white learning spaces. The women's stories also reflect the two parts of my experience as a Black girl in higher education: overachievement that doggedly forced hesitant white allies to underwrite my acceptance in the place and my willingness to acquiesce to expectations of white educational performance, passing as the proper college woman I can never truly be.

Black Diseducation

Dr. Crumpler, Anita Hemmings, and Ellen Love broke barriers by attending schools reserved for white students and therefore accessing knowledge and skills purposefully inaccessible to Black people. But that wasn't the only option. By 1870 there were more than a handful of Black colleges and universities opening across the country in an effort to offer Black students the chance at higher education.[10] The Morrill Act of 1862 provided funding and space for land-grant colleges around the country,[11] some of which permitted Blacks to attend. Yet intense segregation and the continued perpetuation of white supremacist ideals led to the second Morrill Act of 1890 requiring states to create separate land-grant institutions in states with segregated public education.[12]

These schools, later dubbed HBCUs, employed the most educated Black people of the time, who were often unable to gain employment elsewhere, thanks to Jim Crow segregation. Students educated at HBCUs, however, were still viewed unfavorably in comparison to those educated at schools like Princeton and Vassar that did not admit Black students, a perception that carries through the twenty-first century. Forcing Black students into segregated schools and then removing the social capital of their education—regardless of the expertise of educators—prevented the connection between education and upward social mobility in America's intensely capitalist economy. The devaluing of Black-centric education is the first step of perpetuating diseducation in Black communities. All-Black segregated schools were structured top to bottom to create educational access where state and federal governments acted purposefully to prevent such equity, but their social worth has always been viewed in comparison to non-HBCUs, continuously undermining their value.

Du Bois intimated in his ongoing analysis of the Negro education that proper educational training is necessary for the survival of Black communities, lest the post-emancipation Black community, devoid of resources, in need of work, and without true American citizenship, die out completely.[13] On the precipice of a technological and economic revolution, Du Bois warned that without access to formal educational training, Black people sacrifice economic, political, and thus national power for centuries. He wasn't wrong. Our educational achievement has been permanently stunted. Even as we share stories of Black essentialism that detail those successful and often lucky enough to succeed despite the institutional roadblocks set out to prevent their achievement, our success has never signaled a shift in the culture and structure of higher education to increase Black engagement in campus communities.

In general, higher education has failed in its promise to uplift and enhance us. While Du Bois acknowledged the impact of vocational schools and HBCUs, he also understood the cultural affinity to places offering equity in a larger community that does not. Du Bois saw the possibility for racial uplift work as centered in the educational sphere and withstanding the brutality of the white gaze in historically white-serving spaces as the duty of Black students to ensure communal social progress.

In my experience, the benefit of a being educated at highly rated predominantly white schools is access to networks of professional white men and women, with whom I'd otherwise never connect, mastery of standard English in their preferred colloquial style (in Minnesota, this requires an extra level of learning to speak "Minnesota Nice"), and a solid core to withstand the proverbial kidney shots taken day after day in the form of thinly veiled racism. This is a difficult choice to be sure, but necessary in the fight toward more equitable education, where we feel the same implicit sense of belonging that white students experience everywhere—a necessity for improved knowledge acquisition and creativity in these settings. However, the inherent violence of education for Black people cannot be ignored. Radical Black feminist sociology demands an acknowledgment of forgotten narratives of Black education, ignorance of which perpetuates ideologies of education disassociation in Black communities.

Belonging and achievement are perpetually entangled in the institution of education. A sense of belonging among peers and teachers in the classroom stimulates engagement, confidence, and focus in students.[14] Black students, especially in historically white-serving schools, rarely have the opportunity to feel innate belonging. Therefore, our likelihood of achievement is stunted even before our potential is fully evaluated. We have effectively been sentenced to a life littered with institutional barriers, and literal mortal danger, on the road to advanced education.

Young, Black Activism

As the Civil Rights era took hold, and with it organized public protest of Jim Crow laws, colleges and universities, still highly segregated, became ground zero for Black student protests in response to racist campus culture, poor funding of Black programming, and a lack of organizations of interest to Black students. In the winter of 1969, during the frigid spring semester at the University of Minnesota, a coalition of Black students staged a sit-in protest at Morrill Hall, occupying the office of the bursar and records for almost twenty-four hours.[15] Led by Afro-American Action Committee (AAAC) President Rosemary Freeman, a sophomore, and one of only eighty-seven Black students on a campus of 40,000, the organization had communicated their grievances and demands for institutional changes several times previously.[16]

Freeman was originally from Browning, Mississippi, an all-Black community created by a group of ex-slaves shortly after the Civil War. She first came to activism as a high school student working to register Black voters in the south under Martin Luther King Jr. She'd been previously jailed for her participation in voter registration and was therefore no stranger to contentious political situations.[17] The assassinations of Dr. King and then Robert Kennedy in 1968 intensified the AAAC's desire to call the university to action. Among other things, they wanted the institution to foster diversity on campus via scholarships for local Black high school students and the creation of an African American Studies department.

University of Minnesota President Malcolm Moos, previously radio silent in response to the committee's outreach, negotiated a common ground to end the protest by the deadline. And thanks to the action of the AAAC, an African American Studies department was created and the university opened its doors more readily to local Black talent.[18] In February 2019, the University's Department of African American and African Studies celebrated the fiftieth reunion of the protest with teach-ins at the student union, the first time for a public reckoning of the events of 1969. Rosemary Freeman, along with John Wright, Horace Huntley, and Warren Tucker Jr., are rarely known. As the AAAC president and, as she tells it, the one who leveled the playing field between herself and President Moos by greeting him in his own office chair during negotiations, Freeman's involvement is often glossed over in the scant number of available retellings.

When I started my doctoral work in the sociology department at the University of Minnesota almost exactly forty years after the Morrill Hall Takeover (as it has come to be known), I'd never heard the story, nor did I understand the legacy of Freeman's leadership. Which stories get told impact who is able to feel empowered by them. The erasure of Black women's stories weakens our understanding and connection to the legacy of Black women's accomplishments and dims the possibility of our collective strength.

Fifteen years before the Morrill Hall Takeover, the National Association for the Advancement of Colored People (NAACP), working with Black families around the country, brought local lawsuits against counties across the South after being blocked from enrolling their children, mostly Black girls, into segregated white schools, culminating in the landmark Supreme Court case that legalized educational desegregation.[19] The stories of coordinated legal action are rarely heard, silencing the voices of all those other families who sacrificed themselves for the integration fight but whose names are absent from historical narratives on the issue. *Brown v. Board of Education* has been watered down to focus on one little girl, Linda Brown, wiping away what was actually a long-term, strategic plan between the NAACP, more than a dozen families, and the students themselves. This organized erasure of complex political protests organized in Black communities maintains perceptions of our ineptness in political organizing.

It is not a coincidence that girls and women (often mothers and teachers) led the fight for school desegregation. Black girls learn early in life that they will be expected to be poised and strong-willed in the face of danger and degradation. The girls on the front lines of desegregation were physically and psychologically attacked, ignored, or otherwise pushed to their limits at school. In response, their voices were their weapons. They utilized silence when deliberately provoked and spoke up in classes where teachers ignored their signals to participate voluntarily. They endured, sure, but they also made waves.

So much of the work of political organizing and protest has been concentrated among Black girls, in schools.* But to highlight our

---

* In 1963, 600 students (some as young as nine years old) in Birmingham, Alabama, were arrested after walkouts to participate in the sit-ins in segregated spaces across town. They would remain in jail for 10 days (Levingston 2018). The same year, more than a dozen Black girls, ages 12 to 15, were jailed for attempting to use the whites-only entrance at a school field trip to a local Americus, Georgia, movie theater. The girls were held for over eight weeks in a makeshift jail, the location of which was unknown to their parents, where they had little food and lived in squalor. Esty-Kendall, Jud and Emma Bowman. "'I Gave Up Hope': As Girls, They Were Jailed In Squalor for Protesting Segregation," Morning Edition, NPR. https://www.npr.org/2019/01/18/685844413/i-gave-up-hope-as-girls-they-were-jailed-in-squalor-for-protesting-segregation

skills of organization and execution of activism is to magnify our strengths, so the strategy and forethought of Black activism must be repackaged as insignificant or nonexistent. I didn't know my own connections to the desegregation movement until recently, which is perhaps to say I didn't know my strength.

Three years after the *Brown v. Board of Education* decision, The Little Rock Nine, nine Black students—six girls and three boys—enrolled at the all-white Little Rock Central High School just a few blocks from where my mother lived with her family in Arkansas. Just a toddler at the time, my mother and her siblings were often under the care of fifteen-year-old, Carlotta (Walls) LaNier, the youngest of the Little Rock Nine attempting to integrate the local high school and the first Black woman to graduate from Little Rock Central High School.[20] Carlotta was my family's regular babysitter; she was also on the front lines of American desegregation. She, along with her eight classmates, withstood the racial slurs and threats of physical violence in the name of education. She also paid a heavy price. After her graduation, the Walls family was forced to relocate to Colorado to find work and avoid the backlash caused by Carlotta's participation in the equal education fight. Ms. LaNier was a woman I'd never heard directly linked to my family until recently, when I made the decision to uncover her story as a part of ours.

History, as a discipline and a social construct, does not view women, especially Black women, as historical actors. Despite our accomplishments, what we do is not often chronicled as "real" history. This is as true at Vassar as at any other HWSCU. In 1969 and again in 1990, Black students protested on campus and occupied buildings to demand fair treatment and increased support structures for Black students. In 1969, thirty-four Black women undergrads took over the main building in the early morning hours, a result of detailed tactical planning, which allowed them to take over the switchboard with relative ease. They remained for three days until then President Alan Simpson responded to their demands.[21] In February 1990, a group of Black students again staged a sit-in at the main building, this time to protest the hiring of Daniel Patrick Moynihan—a white Republican sociologist infamous for his racist theories about the status of Black communities—as a distinguished lecturer at the college.[22] Moynihan quit his post as a result of the protests.[23]

Recollection of the events is captured in the *Vassar Encyclopedia*, but you won't hear discussions of their organization on campus or about the improvements made as a result of their efforts. There aren't photos capturing their occupation of Main Hall hung alongside those pictures of almost two hundred years of white students that serve as a visual history of the place. There are no anniversary celebrations or well-kept archives of what these students were fighting against or what they achieved. Their stories are functionally lost from the general history of the college.

Black students continue standing on the front lines of protests against police brutality and racism on college campuses across the country. They are being jailed, threatened, and vilified but also ignored in favor of the mainstream appeal of white student activists when the topic is appropriately "non-racial." On college campuses, Black students are challenging their "othered" status in ways I never thought possible. Conservatives often perpetuate the false narrative that colleges are places where hyper-liberal professors hijack students' minds with impractical, politically correct ideals. In reality, my students, mostly Black women, come to me not initially looking to protest. They want to belong, to be the proverbial Vassar girls their white counterparts are offered the chance to become. And they are frustrated that the promises of higher education don't seem to apply to them.

We are not so different, my students and me. Protest is a last resort, a desperate act from groups of people without access to conventional support, but also with limited information about the activism of their forbearers. These Black women want an education free from all the trappings of white supremacy that limit their potential. I didn't protest when I probably should've. I didn't recognize my connections to Black women activists and disruptors of the past, but they were there to be heard. And so, I try to pass down these stories as bits of wisdom from the ancestors I wish I'd had.

A Cultural Career

Should a Black woman make it through the gauntlet of higher education, many end up back in the classroom as teachers. As one of the few non-domestic jobs available to Black women post-emancipation, there is a long tradition of teaching among Black women,[24] including in my own family. Black women's willingness and ability to educate have long been the backbone of Black educational communities, but their occupations also made them dangerous and unpredictable to everyone else.[25] The imagery of educated Black women positions us as villains and reframes our education as a negative characteristic, unlike that of any other demographic. Men call us arrogant, and white women call us confrontational; both detest our continuing overt defiance of racial codes on which American society is balanced. One story my grandmother did tell often was about how much she hated working as a substitute teacher. Her identity as a Black woman of diminutive height (at less than five feet tall) and in the role of substitute teacher meant students tried her in ways they didn't try the white teachers, effectively making her miserable. It would take me thirty-five years, long after she'd passed away, to truly understand her plight, what it meant to be her in those classrooms. Another set of stories, untold.

Recently, as I wandered through a photography exhibit of famous artists' paint palettes, I found myself drawn in by the haphazard distribution of colors across wood characteristic of many pieces in the exhibition. I lingered at these pictures, scanning the smatterings of paint for patterns, some clear organizational structure by which to understand the artists' processes. Paul Cézanne, the French post-impressionist, was one of the few whose layout I understood implicitly. I didn't linger on his palette because the straight-to-the-point approach to blending color and comparing tone felt familiar to me. There was little abstraction to consider and no underlying wildness to unpack. I realized amid the art that I'd been trained to look for patterns.

As a sociologist, of course, my job is to identify and explain patterns in social life and among social groups that give some insight into the interconnectedness of society. Still, long before I declared my major and found my intellectual desires piqued by the discipline, I learned to identify patterns to inform my social interactions. It is in a search for patterns—to explain my own traumas—that I realized what scripts I've followed and why, especially at school. I learned that Black girls in white spaces are expected to engage in an intricate social dance to ensure public acceptance. It's a dance I've come to understand too well—and that learning started before I ever understood the patterns at play.

The usefulness of storytelling to establish connections, instill confidence, and impart knowledge to the audience is well studied.[26] But the trauma of education, the immediacy of basic survival, and for many, stunted communication skills, mean countless stories go untold in Black communities. Some of us, like me, don't know what they're missing. My time on the other side of the educational wall has offered an opportunity to highlight all of the ways I've distorted my behavior, speech, and work to accommodate the assumptions of white peers and make my presence more palatable to their inherently racist sensibilities, the result of years of educational assimilation demanded of Black students to impersonate belonging in historically white-serving schools. But it's also made creative thinking more difficult, a taxing endeavor in an arena where my ideas are often construed as a political ideology, where my freedom of thought is confronted like a weapon in the hands of someone too unstable, incapable of correctly wielding it.

And as I wandered through the art, my recognition of the unfamiliarity of such freedom—to think and create without normalized structure or function—was never clearer. I wasn't born with an innate disinterest in creativity or free thought; it was socialized out of me as I acquiesced to a white educational world. I looked for patterns as a means of survival, in part because I'd only heard stories about the bad things that happen to Black kids who don't. And though I don't want to admit to being *that* little girl, the one who assimilated to survive—I have been.

How might the repetition of the names and stories of Black women in education and the tumultuousness of their paths have helped me face my own? Hindsight is certainly the devil with which we all deal, but I can't help but wonder how I might have fared with such information, if I had heard those stories. I made it to the highest reaches of academia, but paid a physical, psychological, and financial price. I understand my education makes people uncomfortable, and often overextend myself to try to recoup some of that comfort for my oppressors. But this cannot be the end of my story. I'm writing this book to make sure that's not the end of my story, and perhaps to help reestablish Black women as truly belonging in academia in an effort to convince myself.

3

The Disappearance
of Black Teachers

"There's literally more that these students need than I can really give," my cousin, Kim, lamented as we made a late-night run to the store. She was, at the time, a middle school teacher in Houston, and we were sharing our experiences in two very disparate teaching environments. "Half my students need me to speak English and the other half need to hear directions in Spanish," Kim continued. "Wow," I responded, truly shocked. I may have a student or two each year for whom English is a second language, but half the class—of middle-schoolers? "I don't have that problem," I said flatly. "All my students are white."

We laughed together at the joke, understanding the truth behind the humor. Obviously, not *all* my students are white, but enough are upper middle class white kids who easily speak English and would never understand the conundrum of Kim's students, that it often feels like *all* of my students are white. The irony that I'm employed to teach a predominantly white class of students is in how unexpected I am at the head of the class. I'm the one in the room with the doctorate, but my students expect me to *prove* my ability as a teacher to their satisfaction. Both Kim and I are unexpected in the classroom. We share the burden of proof to convince—albeit in different ways—students, other teachers, and administrators that we are capable teachers in these environments, specifically because we're Black.

I come from a long line of teachers, but that—like the revelation that many of my ancestors attended institutions of higher learning—is a fairly recent discovery. My grandmother's retellings of her days as a substitute teacher aside (which were always hilariously bitter), there's been few mentions of our lineage as teachers, and little familial discussion about teaching as a serious occupational choice. Both of these things—the high number of women family members who've worked as teachers at some point in their lives and the absence of familial discussions about that fact—are not shocking revelations about any Black family. Teaching, like clerical work, has historically been a white-collar occupation accessible to Black women and provides access to a middle-class lifestyle and learning. Yet in 2015–2016, Black teachers made up less than 8 percent of public school teachers[1] and Black professors less than 5 percent of university faculty.[2] The teachers in my family were part of the Black teacher force displaced in droves beginning in 1954,[3] but four of my grandmother's sixteen grandchildren became teachers anyway, almost as if it were in our blood.

Pre-desegregation, Black communities across the country created quality all-Black schools led by all-Black teachers and developed pipelines of Black students to college who were then recruited to teach in the very schools they attended as children. Perhaps the most revered of these schools was Dunbar High School in Washington, DC.[4] Established in 1870 as the Preparatory High School for Colored Youth before its renaming for the Black poet Paul Laurence Dunbar in 1916, it was the first nonwhite high school in the United States. Its first class was forty-five students and had only one teacher.[5] That teacher, Emma J. Hutchins, educated all of Washington, DC's Black students after desegregation was struck down in the capitol. As the school expanded, so too did its illustrious staff of Black teachers and principals, as well as the achievement of its students.

Mary McLeod Bethune founded the Daytona Literacy and Industrial Training School for Negro Girls in Daytona Beach, Florida, in 1904.[6] Seeing education as a tool for racial uplift, she created the school to produce a new generation of educated Negro women. At the time, Daytona's education was punishingly and purposefully unequal, where inadequate systems left no viable schooling options for Black students. Bethune's school flourished for almost twenty years before merging with the nearby Cookman Institute, the first HBCU in the state of Florida, to form the HBCU, Bethune Cookman College (now University). The roots of this university sound very similar to my own alma mater, with an original focus on uplifting women through education, albeit white women. And as I researched Bethune's legacy, I couldn't help but wonder if Bethune-Cookman would've been a better place for me,* a Black girl, to learn—a place with a specific history of teaching Black girls.

The tradition of Black intellectualism in the United States, though often ignored, would seem to suggest a time period of increased educational access in Black communities. And wasn't *Brown v. Board of Education*, with all its associated fanfare, supposed

---

* I did know about Spelman College as a similar option when I was applying to colleges, but the Jack & Jill community so prevalent there was not mine.

to close whatever gap existed between the education of Blacks and whites? Instead, Black students are still underrepresented in advanced placement classes and overrepresented in detention. Black people have tried to stake a claim on education, regardless of the consequences, and we have been consistently beaten back. Our cultural thirsting for knowledge is portrayed instead as cultural indifference to it. This deliberate shift of the narratives leaves many Black students feeling lost in academic settings where we should feel self-assured.

No matter how many degrees I have, the feeling of non-belonging remains. I have a doctorate and still have to defend my expertise so often—sometimes hourly—that it feels like a second job. Whenever imposter syndrome shows up, promising that I'll fail, that I'm wholly unqualified to be an academic, as it inevitably does with every article rejection, nasty student evaluation, or just most mornings I wake up for work, I have to remind myself that the very fact of who I am and what I do is a social and political miracle. Black people hold less than 5 percent of doctoral degrees in this country,[7] a statistic too small to be an accident. I feel unworthy or unwanted in my work as an educator and a writer. And it's worth noting, not just for my own self-esteem, that these spaces are built expressly to remind us Black people of our non-belonging via laws and policies written to prevent our entry. To feel like an imposter as a Black woman is a foundation of public education in the United States, a weapon created to maintain appearances as institutions tout equal opportunity while wearing Black students down enough to suppress the meager advances in a ball of self-doubt, self-censorship, and insecurities. I'm here because I belong here, but it rarely actually feels so.

From the moment my ancestors were kidnapped, imprisoned, and forcibly dragged from the coasts of West Africa to the newly formed United States, their education was a criminal offense. Post-emancipation, the *Plessy v. Ferguson* Supreme Court decision in 1896 legalized segregation, including in public schools.[8] The ruling meant that while it was unconstitutional to legally prevent the education of Black people, it was constitutional to segregate Blacks and whites in school (and everywhere else). The Supreme Court, as a reminder of the racist foundations of the formation of America, upheld the constitutionality of segregated public facilities under the guise of separate but equal. This mantra would be repeated to justify the degradation of an entire race of people, but its promises never solidified into institutional change. And so, as modern America was formed around literacy, education, and capitalism, Black people were legally shut out of the process.

An educated Black populace was long feared in the United States, such that our education was made criminal, and when we could no longer be kept from education, we were instead given subpar facilities and supplies. When the first public school for Black students, Hannibal Square Elementary School, opened in Winter Park, Florida, in 1883 it was clear that equal quality and condition was not the goal.[9] The condition of the designated school building was dilapidated, and the books and supplies were tattered hand-me-downs used by white students and then discarded to Black students when their condition made them unacceptable for the former. Public funding for Black schools was scarce, and the entire system seemed hell-bent on dissuading Black people from seeking education at all. Today, Dunbar High School enrolls one thousand students, fewer each year than it did in the 1940s, and instead of developing a network of Black scholars, only about 20 percent of students now meet grade-level reading and math standards. Almost two-thirds of Dunbar's students attended college prior to the school's desegregation; after the school was integrated, its role in providing a premier education to DC's Black students was greatly diminished.[10]

As it became clear that federal and local governments weren't going to provide the resources necessary for the formation of separate but equal learning spaces, Black communities around the country began taking the education of Black people into their own hands, securing the land, constructing the buildings, and funding the cost to run their own schools. Segregated Black schools had limited supplies and teachers, but the influx of Black students never stopped. The strong and continued interest in education—and in higher education—among Black students in these communities encouraged the development of quality Black-only educational institutions at every level. But education was still a difficult institution to enter, and Black students faced arduous and treacherous paths, especially Black women battling racism as well as the structural misogyny that discouraged the education of women of any race. In higher education, often with the help of northern missionary organizations, HBCUs were opened across the southern states, but education, especially for Black girls and women, was still mostly inaccessible.

An Unknown Education Legacy

My maternal grandmother and great-grandmother were educated at Philander Smith College in Little Rock, Arkansas, one of the first schools in the country to accept Black students. It is rare for both of them to have been college educated, considering the time and their complexions, but in many ways I'm still unpacking this legacy. Originally founded as a seminary in 1877, the college was renamed after Smith's widow donated his considerable wealth to the school upon his death. Its connection to the Methodist Church, of which my grandmother was a faithful member during the early years of her life,* provides additional context for the admittance to the school. But these are more details I had to unearth. My great-grandmother was an Eastern Star, a female member of the Freemasons, and a property owner. Her death certificate includes her college-educated status as an indication of its importance, but my family never discussed it.

My grandmother, our fiery matriarch and the woman whose name I bear, left home in small-town Arkansas for the big city of Little Rock at fourteen years old and would go on to attend college before a growing family made it more important for her to be at home. I never saw her as the educated woman she was because no one spoke of it as an accomplishment. Nine children and almost eighteen years after completing her college degree, she reentered the workforce as a substitute teacher, but her educational achievements were forgotten—left behind with little impact on her children. My ancestors' narratives in school didn't fade because they were unaccomplished, but because no one valued their stories enough to understand their power and the potential strength they might instill in their descendants. Perhaps if I'd made connections much sooner between my interest in learning, my preoccupation with school, and specific members of my own family—a bloodline that demonstrated belonging in the classroom—I might've been able to claim a small bit of their legacy for myself. I'd have it to shield my own self-esteem and self-concept to attain academic success without all of the trauma attached. Instead, I was met with disdain in spaces where I pursued these interests with little perceived support to justify and solidify my presence. But it seems those women, women

---

* Leah helped found a local AME church in Little Rock.

like my great-grandmother, Alberta, and my grandmother, Leah, struggled with their identity as educated Black women just as I do.

At a time when home, family, and especially motherhood were the most important cultural features, education got second billing for many Black women. Their college educations also didn't seem to change their lives or the lives of their children dramatically. Education doesn't provide the same return on investment of generational upward social mobility it promises to white students. That it might is one of the great lies of American meritocracy. The early, idealized vision of America touted equal opportunity as the foundation of American exceptionalism. "Any American" can be successful, so theoretically, citizens *should* achieve more because—via education—we have endless opportunities. In reality, those opportunities for upward social mobility, to create stable lives for American families, only existed—in totality—for white men.

The myth of education as the great equalizer was the basis of desegregation advocacy by the late 1950s and at the center of the Supreme Court decision in *Brown v. Board of Education*. By the case's 1954 decision, it was already clear that access to quality education was an important ingredient in the recipe for upward social mobility. For Black people, being denied access to education of similar quality to whites created additional legally mandated barriers to better lives; lives more like those of the white people around them who were being provided institutional support to jump-start a legacy of wealth and prosperity. A surface reading of the fewer than five thousand Black veterans who used their GI Bill on a college education might assume a cultural difference in focus on education, but stories from Black GIs reveal that many Black people who sought higher education with full funding were prevented from enrolling at HWSCUs in the years following their return from war. As a result, a majority of Black veterans used their GI Bills to enroll in HBCUs. Vassar, my alma mater, registered 170 World War II veterans attending on GI Bills between 1948 and 1953. All of them were white.

Education does not impact our ability to make more and have more than our parents in a vacuum. A 2014 study of intergenerational mobility in the United States identified five categories correlated to one's likelihood of moving up the income ladder in their lifetime.[11] These categories, (1) residential segregation, (2) existing income inequality, (3) better schools, (4) social capital, and (5) family stability, are interrogated by spatial difference rather than social.[12] The researchers did not discuss causal connections between these factors, instead focusing on the geographic dynamics of parent and child income. The characteristics of where students live and learn are explained by either lower incomes among the families of Black children compared to white children or lower upward social mobility for all families in areas with a higher percentage of Black people. A focus on geography ignores race-based explanations for lower upward social mobility in areas with higher Black populations. In reality, Black families have lower incomes than white families because they and/or their parents grew up in mostly Black neighborhoods where incomes are depressed, schools are underfunded and understaffed, and families are "disjointed" by mass incarceration and constant state surveillance. These differences are not biological or geographical phenomena, as we were led to believe for so long. It is a result of purposeful structural mandates to degrade collective cultural growth in Black communities.

Segregation, income inequality, schooling, social capital, and family structure are all interrelated mechanisms whose roots can be found in the federal government. For forty years, banks were legally allowed to suppress mortgage approvals, home values, and interest rates in federally "redlined," mostly Black, neighborhoods.

This policy, starting with the Fair Housing Act of 1934,[13] aggravated pre-existing decay of inner-city neighborhood capital. Once the hub of wealth and status, cities were redlined as a tool for racial discrimination and segregation, all but corralling poor and lower middle class Black people in inner cities with poor schooling, depressed home values, and limited job prospects. For thirty-one years, the fate of most Black folks in the United States was legally dependent on access to homes, jobs, and schools outside the inner city. It's no coincidence that my mother headed for the white suburbs from North Minneapolis—which is still home to a majority of Black communities in the Twin Cities—as soon as the opportunity allowed. It was the only way she could see out the of the government-mandated darkness. There's also little doubt that my ability to go from public school to doctorate as a Black woman is in part because of her shrewd choices throughout my childhood education.

Schools exist at the center of the struggle for upward social mobility, to make more and have more than your parents, but the best schools are often out of reach for most Black students. Because public school funding is connected to local and state property taxes, policymakers (via redlining) can perpetuate social class without ever mentioning race. The relative stability of property taxes even in economic downturns when other types of tax (like income and sales taxes) prove volatile makes it a better source of revenue when setting and implementing public school budgets—insulating its use against claims of racism. But it also means that public school funding and budgeting is directly connected to home values in the neighborhoods they serve. By legally allowing mortgage lending banks to connect loan approvals and property valuation to the racial makeup of a city, American politicians doomed Black kids across the country to subpar education. Today Black students are overrepresented in high-poverty schools, perpetuating centuries-old institutionally mandated Black poverty.

Public Education

Before the Civil War, few Blacks in the South (where we were disproportionately concentrated thanks to slavery) received any education at all. Without an established public school system even white children were only educated privately and at a premium. During Reconstruction, public school systems were conceived of, established, and maintained by whites. Their disinterest in providing Black students with similar quality education to white students was clear from the lack of maintenance and support for Black schools. Blacks-only public schools were treated as recycling bins for white schools to discard unused or unwanted public school spaces, supplies, and staff.

While Black educational systems previously subsisted quite successfully with support from Northern abolitionists, Quakers, and other religious organizations, formalizing public school education as state and federal institutions left the education of Black students in the hands of white politicians and administrators who were uninterested in their effective education or potential for academic achievement. Many Black folks in the South were therefore initially in favor of segregated all-Black schools. In the minds of local Black leadership across the South, segregated schools meant control over schools' structures and the education of its students. With a majority of Black teachers and administrators and support from Northern whites sympathetic to the cause, Black organizers felt it was better to maintain distance from "white education" and likewise maintain responsibility for the educational quality of their children.

Unfortunately, access to the necessary financial, administrative, and social support for long-term maintenance of Blacks-only education in the face of a growing white public school system was difficult. The establishment of white Southern Democrats at the beginning of the twentieth century and their renewed commitment to maintaining Black subjugation meant the legalization of segregated schools. They provided a political platform for perpetuating the second-class citizenship of Black people, primarily via education and subsequently by employment as well. Making segregation a legal mandate made it difficult for previously self-segregated all-Black schools to maintain quality education for Black children.

One of the many reasons my grandparents joined masses of other Black people living in the Jim Crow South and headed north, moving their young children from Little Rock, Arkansas, to Milwaukee, Wisconsin, in 1959 was because of the violence and vitriol Black students in their neighborhood experienced during the integration of Little Rock high schools. Around the country, white people gathered each weekday morning to spew racist remarks at the students as they entered integrating schools. Public schools became a purposeful reminder of Black people's second-class citizenship. Across the South, resources were stripped, schools were closed (and would only sometimes reopen—always in poorer than previous conditions), crowding Black children in small schools with few resources in neighborhoods being forcibly transformed into Black ghettos with the government's blessing. As a result, public education became a vehicle for linking class and race, dooming Black people to perpetual poverty in the United States, purposefully passed off as innate.

Carlotta, as my mom and her siblings knew her, was the youngest of the Little Rock Nine but also the first Black woman to graduate from Little Rock Central High School after completing her coursework on-site after the other five women either transferred or completed coursework through the mail to avoid the daily violence imposed upon them by white parents and students.* The situation at Little Rock Central became so untenable in September 1958, just one-year post-integration, that Arkansas Governor Orval Faubus not only postponed integration in the state, he also ordered the closure of all four public high schools in the area to avoid executing federal law. The choice resulted in the "Lost Year,"[14] preventing school for all students rather than allowing Black and white students to be taught together.

Black people aren't born with a natural propensity for poverty. It's not cultural or biological. Our severely limited access to upward social mobility it not a coincidence. It is preset. As early as 1931, the federal government legally mandated the crowding of Black people into urban neighborhoods standing idly by as economic value was sapped from the areas, and school systems degenerated in their wake. My grandparents, with their eldest children primed to enter high school themselves, understood that remaining in Little Rock was dooming them to the same violence experienced by Carlotta and the rest of the Little Rock Nine. So they headed north in hope of a few more opportunities and—they thought—a little less racism, at the very least tolerable schools for their own "nine."

Educated Black folks like Du Bois believed education was the gateway to increased political representation and full civil rights

---

* Elizabeth Eckford and Thelma Mothershed-Wair completed their high school degrees via correspondence in 1958. Minnijean Brown-Trickey was expelled in spring 1959 for calling a group of white students who'd been physically and verbally assaulting her "white trash." Melba Pattillo Beals moved to California in 1959 to live with a white family and finish high school after the local Ku Klux Klan chapter publicized a $10,000 bounty for her murder. Gloria Ray Karlmark finished high school in Kansas City, Missouri, where her family moved during "The Lost Year."

and protested strongly against educational inequality, among other things. The call for desegregation was steeped in this understanding. That Black people would never have an opportunity for success as long as their education was separate from whites was the first and most important reason to attempt to legally force desegregation. It didn't have to be this way; Black communities had developed successful and effective all-Black schools, but a few would never be enough. And so the calls for school desegregation continued.

Promises

The spirit of desegregation was focused on the upward mobility of Black communities. Give us equal access to education and watch us soar! Starting as early as 1934, lawyers for the NAACP began bringing local lawsuits regarding equal access to schooling under the law, arguing that race was not a constitutionally acceptable reason to deny high-quality education to Black students, as the gap between educational settings and opportunities became a gulf. By 1950, most all-Black schools in the South were in complete disrepair.

Racist southern congressmen used public school budgets to depress graduation and retention rates in Black neighborhoods and perpetuate the culture of poverty narrative used to justify their subjugation. Overcrowded, even as the number of Black students compared to white students was small, less than 20 percent of Black high school aged children were actually enrolled in school, and local governments spent almost ten times as many public dollars per white student in comparison to Blacks.[15] *Brown v. Board of Education* was to be a landmark decision, one that would positively alter the lives of every Black person looking to educate themselves. As

Du Bois predicted, the doors were "thrown open for all races," yet the education received in return was quite "pitiable" indeed.[16]

Despite the need for a second Supreme Court decision ordering schools to integrate "with all deliberate speed" in 1955 after schools in many districts purposefully dragged their feet to comply with the law, schools across the South were open to Black and white students equally. All schools were required to meet minimum thresholds for Black and white students based on the racial makeup of the neighborhood, a loophole that threatened to close some of the best all-Black schools in the nation. Meanwhile, racist policy-makers in many states shuttered thousands of all-Black schools in favor of integrating their white counterparts instead. As as result, almost 50 percent of Black teachers and educators across the country were laid off and never rehired into integrated schools. An estimated 40,000 Black teachers were forcibly removed from the educational landscape and never replaced.[17] Academic faculty and administration across grade levels and institutional types have been overwhelmingly white ever since, at the expense of Black students.

The absence of Black teachers in the classroom means informational instruction without cultural connection is a normal experience for Black students. White teachers come to the classroom preprogrammed to expect deviance from Black children they've never met; they expect lazy writing and weak critical analysis before Black students have written a word. In short, they come ready to ignore the needs and possibilities of their Black students, delegitimizing the very education they're tasked to provide, and robbing Black students of equitable education even as they share classrooms with white students. Black teachers are more likely to advocate for Black students, more likely to point out personal impacts on classroom behavior before unnecessary disciplinary action, and more likely to present content in a way that is digestible for Black students. But we are less than 7 percent of the teaching force at all levels and types of non-HBCU schools. The removal of Black teachers in white schools preserves our institutional isolation in academic spaces.

When Malvern Colored High School and A.A. Wilson High School, the two "colored" schools in Malvern, Arkansas—the small town outside of Little Rock where my grandmother was born and raised—merged in 1970 as a part of integration efforts, the community lost an entire school and many Black teachers in the process. My great-aunt Henrietta, a teacher at Malvern Colored High School, and her husband, Edward, the school's principal, were offered teacher and assistant principal roles at the integrated school. While they were allowed to continue post-integration, perhaps because of their matching master's degrees from Columbia University's Teacher's College, their roles were diminished with the closing of their all-Black school despite the years of energy and effort the couple spent maintaining the quality of education there.

Many public schools in the South, like Dunbar High School, saw the quality of education drop so low that those who could afford it—mostly white families—withdrew their students in large waves from local public schools and enrolled them in private schools. In Arkansas, Alabama, and Virginia, lawmakers wrote manifestos lamenting desegregation and passed laws to close schools rather than integrate them. The move to close schools or degrade public school quality precipitated the development of a two-tier system of education at the K through 12 level. These two tiers, one public and one private, ensure the quality of education received is a direct reflection of how much your parents can afford to segregate your schooling among the white and wealthy, either via high tuition at private schools or high home prices and property taxes in towns with quality public schools.

Today, many students forced to study in re-segregated schools face the daily trauma of subpar education from those least concerned with, or supportive of, the academic achievement of Black students. What are the results of this trauma? In all of the Instagram montages of Black undergrads, graduate students, med students, and law students, we see the smiling faces of the Black educated populace. Amid the fierce Black girl magic dripping from their monochromatic photo sessions in bathing suits, white coats, and ball gowns, the trauma of what they've undertaken is invisible. Increases in our advanced education mean simultaneous increases in self-reported mental, physical, and emotional stress.[18] We're improving our educational capital, but not our financial or social capital. And at what cost?

Expected Disrespect

"He said *what* to you?" My mom refused to let me continue, interjecting as I relayed the events of that afternoon's meeting with my guidance counselor to her. "He called my list *ambitious*," I repeated, being sure to emphasize the final word and convey the lack of respect with which he said it. "*Excuse me*," my mom responded, less a question directed at me and more a retort of disgust at this man's words. Truthfully, I'd half-hoped, half-expected this response, and spent the rest of the afternoon crafting the right words to ensure my guidance counselor could expect a visit from my mother. I smiled at the thought of him receiving my mother's ire as she advocated for me, the overachiever who, if I were white, would be applauded for my hard work rather than insulted in the face of it.

"His job isn't even to judge the *ambitiousness* of your list," my mother continued. "His job, if he cares to do it, is to explain the application process." "Which is pretty self-explanatory," I chimed in. These are some of my favorite moments with her, us bonding over the disrespect of white people, providing opportunities for me to watch my mother's responses and carefully note her successful techniques. This wasn't the first time we'd had a problem at this new school, either, so my mother was primed to bring our grievances directly to the source. "Right," she agreed. "Tomorrow, I'll take you to school and let this man know what I expect from him in regards to your college applications: not much."

The next day Mom followed me to school in her own car to meet with said counselor before work. I wasn't allowed to attend the meeting with her, it was grown folks' business after all, but I never had another meeting with him again. When I asked her about it later that night at home, she only said, "It's handled. You will apply to the schools we agreed on. You don't have to worry about him." I needed that protection. I recognize now, as an adult, just how much my mother shielded me from. I needed her shield much longer than I think she realized.

The list of fifteen schools where I'd potentially spend the next four years of my life was negotiated carefully between me and my mother. It reflected my academic achievements, attraction to warm-weather climates, and disinterest in staying in the Midwest. My mother insisted on a big list of schools so as to gauge the market. I wasn't going to suffer from too many choices, but I could be easily derailed by too few, she reasoned. So, I knew even before this conversation that she'd be particularly affronted by his dismissiveness of the list she'd basically curated.

It wasn't a shock to me or my mother that my desire to apply to prestigious colleges was challenged by white educators. By seventeen years old, I'd come to expect, and was learning how to confront, discrimination and racism in a variety of environments, but at school, interactions felt particularly egregious. School integration, as a symbol of progress in the Civil Rights Movement, superseded the importance of cultural connections and mentorship needs of Black children in the classroom. Perhaps those advocating hardest for the passage of desegregation policies didn't realize this, or truly believed that the goal of educating white and Black children together would not lead to the isolation of Black students at school. Either way, forcing Black students into white schools committed to maintaining educational distance between Black and white students created a structural and cultural cycle of Black academic isolation. It represents the beginning of modern Black diseducation.

Black academic isolation negatively impacts the mental health of Black college students in historically white-serving environments. Academic success at all levels is attained in part via hard work and persistence and an ability to withstand violence in the classroom. Black students being taught by white teachers in classrooms filled with mostly white students means that the potential for imposter syndrome is high and instigated by lowered expectations of ability and predetermined expectations for Black students compared to their white peers. It starts with little comments like that of my high school counselor, which implied that I didn't belong in prestigious institutions and ends in institutional violence.

The lack of Black advocates in HWSCUs means there is nothing between Black students and the institution itself, which is inherently uninterested in Black student success and run via white supremacist policies. Instead, we've been socialized to understand our existence in education as a lonely one. We have come to expect the experience to be traumatic, punishment for circumventing institutional attempts at Black diseducation. The resulting anxiety and depression from daily exposure to systemic and individual racism have lasting physical and psychological impacts on the lives and futures of Black students.

The issue of trauma as a result of Black diseducation is not limited to our time as students. After graduation, the reality of a perpetual inability of Black students to benefit from the credentials for which they've sacrificed so much of their mental and physical health starts to set in. Because Black people have been reimagined in the American social memory as unlikely to be uninterested in or unable to complete advanced education, highly educated Black folks rarely assume the same kind of capital from their educational training and positions. The social fact of Black diseducation permanently positions Black people as uneducated, forced to justify not just our intellect or interest in learning but also that we've earned any significant status as a result.

The questioning of Black students' accomplishments starts even before questions about college attendance come up. By the time I was a junior in high school, despite my academic achievements, it became standard to question my ability. By the time I finished my doctorate, asserting my achievements, and therefore my ability, was a required part of my daily routine. This unyielding non-belonging in education requires Black academics to constantly reaffirm our credentials to maintain access to predominantly white academic networks and the spaces where those networks are constructed.

In Which We Can't be Doctors

In 2016, Tamika Cross, an OB/GYN from Houston, was traveling to Detroit for a wedding on Delta Airlines flight 945 when a white woman two rows in front of her lost consciousness and flight attendants called for the help of any doctors onboard. The white flight attendant with whom Dr. Cross interacted grilled her for several minutes, ostensibly to confirm her credentials, before deciding to let a white male doctor onboard help instead, implying that she didn't *seem* enough like a doctor to be trusted to help with the present medical situation.[19] Dr. Cross's story is evidence of a distinct pattern of Black de-credentialing today. The flight attendant in question didn't inherently believe Dr. Cross's assertion of her title as a medical doctor because she didn't look the part, unlike the similarly "uncredentialled" white man she ultimately allowed to attend to the unconscious woman. This white woman, the flight attendant at the center of this conflict, is probably not an overt racist—though I reserve the right to be wrong on this point. Instead, the inherent domination of racism is on display as years of socialization told her a Black woman cannot be a doctor.

Dr. Cross is not recognized as a woman with advanced medical credentials because we have a long history in the United States that highlights the high improbability of such a circumstance. Black people are already less than 13 percent of the total population; add to that three hundred years of social, economic, and educational depression through deliberate resource inaccessibility, and the flight attendant's response makes more—albeit institutionally racist— sense. There are almost nine hundred thousand active physicians in this country, and less than 2 percent of them are Black women. The likelihood of crossing paths with one of the less than eighteen thousand Black women doctors anywhere is low, and that's just the way the institution wants it. Dr. Cross isn't perceived as a doctor because, more often than not, doctors are not Black women.

Dr. Crumpler was so skilled that even a board of white men could not deny her accomplishments. But the difficulty of her experiences at the New England Female Medical School is not a story to be told as an admonishment of past racist misdeeds in the United States. It is the beginning of a purposeful pattern created to define the concepts of expertise, education, and intellect along racial lines. Black people cannot be educators or, by extension, experts because we're confined to the uneducated, un-intellectual populace, to be seen and worked, but not heard.

Even when a Black woman's credentials are undeniable, white supremacist education structures her as an enemy to the system—unqualified and untrustworthy. Black women may be earning degrees at our highest rate ever, but we're also still underrepresented in every field of the white-collar landscape.[20] This is especially true of higher education where Black women make up less than 4 percent of all college and university faculty. For the small percentage of us afforded entrance into academia, there awaits a new set of obstacles to hurdle—the racist ideologies of fellow faculty, students, and administrators. Black women faculty are more likely than white women faculty to receive lower teaching evaluation scores, be tasked with burdensome "diversity-related" service responsibilities, and perceived as difficult to work with.

Throughout my high school and college years, as I started to consider careers and adult life, being a college professor was never on my radar. Growing up in the Midwest, I rarely encountered Black teachers—or any who weren't white cis men and women—in the classroom. I never saw teachers who looked like me, so I never perceived teaching, at any level, as something I could actually do. The few Black teachers I did encounter seemed as happy to see me as I was to see them, but they also seemed ill at ease, or perhaps I projected my own feelings onto my perceptions of them. Either way, teaching, especially at the highest level, has always been presented as something for which I was inherently unfit.

That perpetual ideology of educational disparities (in experience and evaluation) created via the innate misfit of Black people and education is by design. For those who breach the ivory walls, more overt tactics are sometimes required. In 1970, before she'd even taught her first class as acting assistant professor of philosophy at UCLA, the university's Board of Regents tried to fire Dr. Angela Davis. A different kind of doctor than Dr. Cross and Dr. Crumpler, but still explicitly unwelcome in higher education, Dr. Davis faced a barrage of attacks on her racial and political identities.

Then California Governor Ronald Regan actively lobbied for her termination from UCLA because of her much-publicized membership in the Communist party before she'd ever even taught a class. Dr. Davis's opening lecture was attended by over two thousand students and had to be moved from its originally scheduled classroom to accommodate the crowd. She'd go on to teach three courses during the 1969–1970 academic year, but Dr. Davis was not reappointed after her contract with UCLA expired.

Dr. Davis did not go quietly. The University of California Board of Regents was censured by the American Association of University Professors for not renewing her contract, a judge ruled that she could not be fired simply for her membership in the Communist party, and she was allowed to resume teaching for a time.[21] However, a few months later, Dr. Davis was again released from her post, and months after that, in August 1970, she'd be implicated in the kidnapping and murder of a judge and two defendants during a California murder trial.[22] Jailed, prosecuted, and later exonerated, Dr. Davis and her connection to the advocation of communism was used first to block her integration into academe and then to proscribe her acumen and subsequent public advocacy as treacherous and she as an arch-enemy of the state. In 1995, she would teach at Vassar College.

In many ways, the political caricature of the villainous intruder, a Black woman student or educator set to upend the delicate balance of white supremacist education, is no different now than it was then. Repeatedly, Dr. Davis was treated as unfit for education.

However, her degree credentials said otherwise. Future president Ronald Regan wanted her fired, but students showed up in droves to support her. She was forced out of UCLA and into the courtroom, but forty-five years later returned to the institution as a professor emeritus, a symbol of the continued resistance, often confused for grit. Black teachers are continually removed from classrooms, but Black women have only increased their matriculation in response. White supremacist institutions will continue trying to keep us out, but we keep showing up, no matter how much trauma is inflicted upon us. We're constantly exposing our bodies to physical and emotional distress—and we are wounded.

Black people are one of the last racial groups granted widespread access to formal education. Still, despite our continued prohibition from education, we were able to create and sustain all-Black schools and a workforce of all-Black teachers for almost eighty years before desegregation became the scapegoat for dismantling our established infrastructure in the name of fairness. We have yet to receive the equality promised to us by *Brown v. Board of Education*. Instead, we are even more displaced and underserved than before the law that was supposed to improve our circumstances was enacted. Black people took intellectual spaces where there were none provided and were later forced to watch as the court system not only took away that infrastructure but restructured the entire institution to ensure that Black people would have difficulty depending solely on public education to achieve any measure of success. A scam from which we continue to be harmed.

4

Racing

I anticipated the approach of the old white woman as my friend and fellow Vassar alumni Pedro and I climbed the stairs of Rockefeller Hall. We were two of a handful of nonwhite alumni leadership attending the weekend's volunteer service conference that brought us back to campus. The woman made eye contact before I even had the opportunity to focus on additional faces in the room and was making her way toward us with the deliberate confidence that only white people can summon. This woman, like many Vassar girls, was small but self-assured, not giving away a hint of the racist statements on the tip of her tongue. I braced myself anyway, just as I do whenever I meet new white people, especially in privileged settings like the one we were in. This was not my first rodeo, though, and a quick scan of the room and the woman approaching me told me that she was about to demand my time and attention to serve her own needs; I, in this public but exclusive setting, had so much more to lose.

"Hi, I'm Gwendolyn," she said, pointing at her name tag. "I was wondering if I could ask you what it was like for you at Vassar." She continued before I even had a chance to offer my name in response. "There weren't many, you know, non-white people here when I was a student," Gwen explained in a whispered tone. "Or men," she adds as Pedro appears at my side.

I stuttered as I began, "Well . . ." I said slowly, stalling, trying to decide the best course of action in this situation. This wasn't a woman with whom I felt safe having frank conversations about my experiences as a Black student at Vassar, but I also didn't want her to leave presuming my racial identity had zero negative effect on my time on campus. And though it was tempting, I resisted the urge to point out the white privilege steeped within her eagerness to ask this deeply personal question of me and the ease with which she had assumed I'd answer. Instead, I plugged this book, dropped my credentials to regain some footing in the interaction, and excused myself quickly before she had the chance to ask the long list of follow-up questions percolating behind her eyes. So I shouldn't have been surprised when six hours later I heard the faint cry of "Ursinus College" (the school where I was faculty at the time) coming from behind me. It was a small snippet of information I'd dropped to assert my belonging and it was now being used to dehumanize me.

I turned, a reflex I'd developed long ago anytime I heard something vaguely connected to facets of my identity—a consequence of years of being addressed by white people by anything other than my actual name—to find Gwen once again demanding my time as she walked more briskly toward me to "remind" me of our earlier conversation. But it was a bigger reminder of how much I stuck out on this campus, as an outsider to be regarded differently, as an "other." In the end, she wanted nothing more than to continue to interrogate me about who I am, what I do, and how I came to attend Vassar. Not because she wanted to know me as a person—a human—but because she clearly could not fathom my membership among alumni at *her* beloved school. Even almost fifteen years post-graduation, in the role of class leader and with a PhD, I'm still just a Black girl at a white school.

Geography Matters

I grew up in Minnesota at a time when there were fewer than fifteen thousand Black people living in the entire state, but my home life was very Black. My parents made sure we were constantly surrounded by extended family and that we were culturally well-developed in terms of our integration into the Black church, our exposure to Black music and Black food, Black hairstyles, and Black art. We played with Black dolls, spent our early summers in a Black Baptist church on the south side of Chicago, and listened to Anita Baker and Luther Vandross as we cleaned the house on Saturdays, but the significance of our race and the social disadvantages built into such a degraded identity were foreign to me until I got to school.

My parents made sure I was educated at the best public schools they could access, but that also meant I attended historically white-serving schools for my entire educational life. Growing up in suburban Minnesota in the 1990s meant I had to be a chameleon, Black and white, culturally speaking, and capable of imperceptibly shifting and switching with the setting. The experience was as socially beneficial as it was traumatic. To be Black, female, and educated in white schools meant my ability was constantly challenged by white teachers, administrators, and guidance counselors, or questioned by Black family members unsure how to respond to— let alone best encourage—my growth. I wanted school to be the place, more than any other, where I was able to forget I was Black, but a level of comfort that allowed me to focus first and foremost on my learning (and then my teaching) was never offered. Instead, school was the place where my racial identity constantly marked me as other, where I was perpetually raced.

I always feel a sense of uncontrollable jealousy when I hear other Black people, those of us who had the fortunate circumstance of growing up in mostly Black—or at the very least, not completely white—middle-class neighborhoods, wax poetic about an upbringing devoid of daily racist interactions and full of cultural support and protection. Such a cocoon of support gives Black children time to grow educationally and emotionally before being forced to confront the global implications of being Black in America. We, who grew up in predominantly white schools with predominantly white teachers, and without the shield of communal Blackness, especially at school, weren't so lucky.

The first person to call me a nigger was a classmate. I was almost eight years old and on my way home from school. I'd just gotten off the school bus and was trudging through the knee-high snow drifts that lined our white suburban neighborhood when a white boy who rode the same bus, and got off at the same stop, pushed me in the back and half-yelled, half-laughed, "Nigger!"

As I fell face-first into the cold, hard, and wet snow, I didn't make a sound. I lay there for a moment, forcing myself not to cry—a skill I was already attempting to master as a sensitive kid prone to crying. My tears, usually the result of anger and frustration, were unwelcome in a family and a community where my emotional control was demanded. That day was no different. I had heard that word before, and though I can't claim to have fully comprehended its weight at the moment, I knew this was happening because I was Black and he was white. I was sure of this fact as much as I was when my teachers feigned trouble pronouncing my name as though it were written in Swahili or when the white girls with whom I often had playdates made me play Ken instead of Barbie because I didn't "look like Barbie" and they did. I knew there was something different about my skin even without the language to describe it clearly.

So I held back my tears, unwilling to provide this kid the satisfaction of knowing how much his actions hurt me. After taking a few moments to compose myself, I pushed my hand deeper into the cold snow, looking for leverage to push my body up and off of the ground. I wiped the snow from my clothes as I regained my footing; then, after figuring that I was physically more or less OK, I continued toward my house. That was twenty-eight years ago, and I still remember every moment.

Going to school with white people was the catalyst for the development of my double-consciousness, the Du Boisian sensation of dividing one's identity into multiple parts, unable to develop a self-concept devoid of white people's perceptions of Blackness perhaps precipitated by that moment in the snow. At school I learned to be both Black and a student, unlikely to exist in academic settings without oppression, and never able to truly be myself. How do my outcomes differ from someone whose double-consciousness development was sparked by experiences from a different institution? How and when does race become salient for a Black child if it's not at school? Ta-Nehisi Coates, in his book *We Were Eight Years in Power*, reveals he "did not understand Blackness as a minority until [he] was an 'only,' until [he] was a young man walking into rooms filled with people who did not look like [him]. In many ways, segregation protected [him]. . ." (p. 52).[1] I can't relate. I've never entered spaces—other than familial—where I wasn't "an only."

I've understood my Blackness as a minority since my first days in my North Minneapolis kindergarten class. At school, I learned that no amount of effort superseded racialized perceptions of me as a Black girl. And that being Black, and a girl, was an undesirable identity to have in these predominantly white schools—as though I could, and should, exchange it for a new, more palatable one. Regardless of my hard work or good grades, no matter the proof of my ability or intellect, my worth and fit were always challengeable in these mostly white educational spaces. I would never really belong.

Structure and Culture

After *Brown v. Board of Education,* you won't find much mention of race in institutional policies—save for short segments about hate speech at the most progressive schools—but racial identity colors everything about an individual's experience in educational institutions. HWSCUs reinforce expectations of Black inferiority and, whenever possible, the erasure of Blackness altogether. Not simply in the classroom but also in both the structures and cultures of schools, race—and gender—hierarchies are learned, shared, and enforced.

While desegregation focused on integrating classrooms, very little attention was paid to anything else. Inclusion into the institutional fabric of those schools was impossible because Black students' perspectives were never incorporated into the institutional plan. We were just ripped from schools that were planned for us and dropped into schools that weren't. Perhaps Du Bois was right to fear integration for Black folks. To be superficially integrated into a place is to be constantly reminded of your objectionable presence. There will always be those who view you as eternally unwelcome. At school, that constant sense of "unwelcomeness" is manifested as imposter syndrome, social isolation, or disengagement from learning, but the goal of structuring education this way is always the same: making knowledge, learning, and school itself inherently white.

In 1969, a group of Black students at Memphis State University protested a continual lack of genuine Black student integration on campus by leading a movement to "Blacken" traditional white campus spaces to which they were usually excluded. Instead of adhering to the status quo, these Black women student activists aggressively campaigned for positions on beauty pageants, homecoming court, the cheer and pep squads, and other organizations, known previously as for white women coeds only.[2] The goal of their expansive protest movement was to highlight how blocking Black students from participation in campus activities kept them disengaged from campus culture. Preventing Black students from participating in these extracurricular activities was not just demoralizing and not only a question of access. The absence of Black women in these spaces perpetuated their erasure on campus.

The inability of these Black coeds to breach the barriers of contests and organizations tasked with setting normative beauty standards, moral service boundaries, and college membership maintains the whiteness of campus and encourages Black students to remain in the margins. If Black women students can't participate in Memphis State beauty pageants, then they have no opportunity to meet (or exceed) normative beauty standards. If they cannot join ROTC,* then they cannot access military benefits and ranks and all the social benefits that arise from membership. If they cannot try out for the campus cheer or pep squads, then they're banned from the institutionalized celebration of college sports and important social gatherings for coeds. Black students cannot be college students in the full sense of the phrase. We can take classes, and even earn a diploma, but Black women are constantly reminded that we'll never belong at school.

---

* Beginning in 1972, women were officially eligible for ROTC membership.

Black diseducation does not just increase Black students' uncertainty about belongingness, it also limits imagery of Black people across the educational culture. In the Memphis State University example, Black diseducation is a concerted effort to cement a concrete incompatibility between Black college students and the culture of higher education, not just in the classroom structure, but in the culture of extracurricular activities, as well—an important integration mechanism for acclimating college coeds.

Fifty years later, school policies targeting Black students continue to remind us that we're just as undesirable in educational spaces as we've always been—from our heads to our feet. In Florida, many schools ban culturally Black hairstyles, including dreadlocks and braids, for students during the school day and those attending school-sponsored activities. The NAACP Legal Defense Fund in 2018 asked the Florida Department of Education to acknowledge the racism in such policies and reprimand schools with Black hairstyle bans.[3] There was no formal response, but Florida legislatures introduced the CROWN (Creating a Respectful and Open World for Natural Hair) Act bill to prohibit hair discrimination in 2019. In July 2022, the bill failed for a third time. It was reintroduced in 2023.

The 11th Circuit Court of Appeals ruled in September 2016 that employers have a legal right to turn away potential employees with dreadlocks,[4] a decision only intensifying arguments that school bans are worthwhile. These policies also reinforce the idea that Black people are to be controlled, that our culture is unwelcome in public spaces—unless it's being commodified—and its presence there must be constrained. Without federal law banning discrimination based on hair texture or style, individual states must pass prohibitive legislation. As of 2022, only twelve states have done so.

School policies like these remind Black students that they are Black before they are students. Their race has more salience than their education, unlike their white peers, who get to be students first and only. Empirical comparisons of retention, graduation, and other educational achievements that ignore that the fabric of academic experiences for Black students are fundamentally different because of the salience of race at school and are therefore invalid.[5] Schools are foundational settings of socialization; they teach us how to act, walk, talk, and think in a narrow, white-supremacist and heteronormative framing. Until a person starts attending school, their basic understanding of self-concept is built on the people and places around them.

At school, however, my Blackness became my defining feature, with my gender not far behind. My identity made me a centerpiece in the classroom, to be regarded as something beyond the expectations of my students and teachers—a barrier to discussions across the classroom table, someone who had to be talked around, over, and through, but rarely engaged directly. I didn't (and still don't) have the luxury of regarding my peers and teachers as unique but unnecessary and removable objects, as they did me. Not unlike the silence I was met with in my sixth-grade science class, my contributions in predominantly white classrooms were often met with little acknowledgment, sometimes even disdain. Interracial engagement with non-Black students was a requirement, not a choice, so I had to learn early on the rules of constant marginalization. I had to learn how my race changed the tenor of my interactions, and I had to learn to deal with racism as a part of my everyday life, even as a part of my learning environment.

My attendance at predominantly white schools throughout my K through 12 education meant my public racing began early. Hyper-visibility in the classroom also left me isolated and subject to constant stereotypical assumptions about my fit, for which I was inherently unprepared. Expectations of my reduced intellectual capacity compared to my white peers as a result of my Black identity meant that assumptions that I was unprepared or uninterested in advanced education were often used intentionally to limit my educational growth (see racist guidance counselor). On several occasions throughout middle school and high school, even before my run-in with the counselor about college admissions, I was counseled not to take accelerated classes—a suggestion that would likely have made my list of potential colleges just as ambitious as my guidance counselor claimed. Instead, my four advanced placement courses should've helped me stand out.

My mother, my first and most steadfast advocate, taught me not to accept racist treatment and was quick to stop by the school to let them know that she wouldn't tolerate her daughter being held back. I understand that I was lucky in this regard. I had a mother who was highly educated, successful, and understood that schools were breeding grounds for racism. She taught me to regard everyone I met in educational spaces with caution, that teachers and counselors don't always have my best interests at heart, and most importantly, to speak up when I felt I was being treated unfairly. I spent this time in school—as my white counterparts started considering their futures and exploring potential micro-identities—learning what it meant to be Black where Blackness was unwelcome. But even those experiences cannot adequately prepare Black students for life at HWSCUs.

Becoming Black on Campus

College is a different animal. During the K through 12 years, I always had my family and extended family to cling to. No matter what happened at school, I returned each day to a home full of

Black people with whom I would laugh and fellowship, others who understood the weight of a day spent as the only Black face in all-white rooms. In college, especially when you're fifteen hundred miles away from your family, a sense of belonging is important. Attending college means living, working, *and* learning in an institutionally racist environment, where a sense of belonging is impossible for Black people. There are few social or psychological protections for a Black student at a white college, and those that exist are oases, water in the interminable desert. And for many Black students, college is the first time we experience such complete immersion, even those of us who went to predominantly white K through 12 schools, but especially those who are entering predominantly white classrooms for the first time and find this sudden and complete immersion in whiteness a shock to the system.

Former first lady Michelle Obama, at stops throughout her husband's 2008 presidential campaign, often talked about the idyllic nature of her home life. Growing up in the South Shore neighborhood of Chicago during the 1970s, Obama (née Robinson) was raised in a home with a stay-at-home mother who was adored by her friends, a father who solely provided for the family, cabin vacations to Michigan, and family nights playing Monopoly (which, if her family is anything like mine, were characterized by a loving intensity that translated to real competition).[6] She, like so many of us, was shielded from the daily horrors of school at home with cultural familiarity and support. But when she arrived at Princeton University in 1981, Obama was confronted with the reality of life at HWSCUs.[7]

"You're at a ten, and I need you at about a three," a group of white peers yelled in my face. They were clearly at about a fifteen, if we're actually comparing volume decibels in any realistic way, but they weren't. These interactions were repeated weekly for four full years at Vassar. They weren't trying to silence me in a literal way, but instead expressed a (perhaps subconscious) desire to control the volume and exuberance of my voice. Something else that felt unique to me at the time were the critiques of Black women as too loud and in need of quieting, long used as a method of informal social control. It's just another way to keep a Black woman in check. It was a signal of non-belonging disguised as an innocent joke, reminding me and everyone else within earshot that I'm an outsider whose volume—unlike their own—needs to be checked because this isn't my space in the same way it's theirs. So, criticism of my volume said "in jest" branded me the loud, unruly Black woman before I actually had a chance to be truly loud or unruly.

At first, I took their criticisms seriously, appalled that I'd so blatantly broken the upper-class expectation of softness and light, the sense of decorum in public settings. But in the midst of this perpetual othering via the perceived unsuitability of my volume I realized that they, just as much as anyone—including me—were loud, brash, and uncouth, but their whiteness shielded them from the same criticism. The same accusations from me about my white peers' volume don't hold the same weight. I was perpetually open to criticism, and they were not.

Differences in on-campus experiences for Black students are historically impacted by perceptions of connections to whiteness. This was especially true at Vassar, the last of the Seven Sisters to willingly accept Black women within their walls. W.E.B. Du Bois personally advocated for Beatrix "Beatty" (McCleary) Hamburg to become the first Black woman* openly admitted to the college.[8] She

---

* Dr. Hamburg, Dr. Christmas, and Camille (Cottrell) Espeut were admitted to Vassar College in rapid succession in 1940–41. Because of World War II, the college accelerated degree progress so students could participate in the war effort. Dr. Hamburg was one of seven seniors awarded diplomas in December 1943 as a part of this acceleration (class of 1944). Dr. Christmas and Camille Espeut graduated as members of the truncated class of 1944–45.

was followed in quick succession by June Jackson and Camille Cottrell. They were light skinned, attractive, and personable, not unlike the characteristics used to describe Anita Hemmings's unassuming Blackness.[9] McCleary was as close to the ideal woman to challenge Vassar's racial barriers and institutional fears of the potential negative impacts on the school's reputation because of her installation on campus. She was chosen explicitly because her Blackness was nonthreatening, but her presence at this all-white school was racialized by the institution itself, despite her so-called palatability.

Michelle Obama's undergraduate thesis "Princeton-educated Blacks and the Black Community" was the source of much political controversy during her husband's 2008 presidential campaign after Republicans tried to use the research focus to expose her Black radicalization. The attempt, while unsuccessful in preventing her husband's ascendance to the presidency, is a common response to Black folks' acknowledgment of the embeddedness of American racism, not just in its people but in the construction of its most fundamental institutions.

At Princeton, Obama was a Black woman first and a student second, regarded as an interloper, and she internalized herself as a "visitor" with little perceived belonging. In the thesis introduction, she grapples with the social consequences of her racial identity in this space. Her experiences are not unexpected for a Black woman at an HWSCU. In my own research on belonging on college campuses, women participants and minority student participants (primarily by race, sexual identity, and religion) reported a weaker sense of belonging than their white and male counterparts. Weak levels of belonging are often associated with specific incidences that highlight an individual's race as the main factor used to characterize belonging, usually precipitated by some tangible experience of racism on campus, and Obama herself has such an experience.

The parents of one of Obama's first-year roommates tried to have their daughter's dorm reassigned rather than have her room with a Black woman. The attempt was unsuccessful, but the message was clear: "You're not welcome here, and I don't want you corrupting the social and academic success of my child."

In an environment where perceived belonging is low and white supremacy is mapped on the institutional walls, space becomes vitally important to long-term survival and success. White students on a predominantly white campus perpetually and unquestionably belong in almost all spaces. Conversely, the "unfriendly Black hotties"[10] of high school become the angry Black militants in college regardless of their actual political ideologies in the eyes of the white students and staff around them. Black students inherently do not belong. Therefore, they likely seek interaction with other Black students and engagement with topics and programs focused on issues important to the Black community. The racialization of college campuses means that processes of integration are weak. Institutional regulation is high, shining a spotlight on the group on campus with the most to lose from failure—Black students—and simultaneously creating an environment that encourages it.

Shaping institutional perceptions of Black students on campus based on the behaviors and statements of individuals turns racism into a people problem rather than a structural or cultural issue, weakening institutional urgency to make institutional changes. The strength and pervasiveness of white supremacy, the entitlement it maps unto white students in predominantly white schools, and the impact on white/Black student interactions within campus communities is thus ignored. To pay it attention, or to consider Black student perspectives in the development of institutional policy or their role in campus culture, would be to acknowledge that Black students on college campuses are subjected to racism in perpetuity—in the classroom, in the dorms, in hook-up culture participation, in administrative discipline, and most importantly, in advising and mentoring. Many colleges are just not ready to admit the inherent trauma of college campuses.

Obama, who was shielded from (some) racism during her upbringing in a diverse Chicago neighborhood, experienced the shock of 24/7 life in a predominantly white institution, but her attendance at more diverse K through 12 schools and an absence of experiences of overt racism pre-college doesn't make her reaction to campus cultural racism unique. Though Black women enter college from a variety of institutions and at annually increasing rates, the misogynoir, that unique kind of racism mixed up especially for Black women that we're confronted with in college, is punishingly similar.

The Other Talk

Recent public awareness of "the talk" Black parents have to give their Black children about interactions with police and assumptions of deviance just for being Black, overshadows the other talk for which Black parents must prepare. This talk focuses on the traumas of hyper-surveillance in Black communities and the communal damage of mass incarceration for Black families. The talk seeks to convey the abject criminalization of Blackness in public life but rarely details the specific forms of racism Black people encounter in different settings. I don't yet have children, but often find myself earnestly organizing the right arrangement of words to convey what I know about the way these structures of domination are set up to encourage our failings. I haven't yet settled on what to say, but the older I get, the more heavily the knowledge weighs on me that the day will come when this discussion will be necessary.

My talk won't just be about fearing the police and any white people who envision themselves civil servants attempting to enforce obscure laws against Black people in public spaces. I want to convey to my children that it's not just formal policing they have to worry about. It will also point to teachers, principals, counselors, friends, and parents of friends as potentially racist. Informal institutional policing at school, with friends, even in friends' homes may also subject them to unexpected violence and other traumas rooted in their racial identity. I want them to be ready.

This other talk tries (and often fails) to explain future disappointments at school and work that will feel in the moment unexplainable. It tries to prepare Black children to have their hard work overlooked, their achievements demeaned, and their credentials ignored. But how do you explain to your child that no matter how hard they work, no matter what they accomplish, success may continue to feel out of reach? The future mother in me often feels paralyzed by the knowledge of the talk's simultaneous impossibility and absolute necessity.

Some version of this talk includes the sentencing of Black people to a lifetime of overwork, undercompensation, and a front-row seat to watch mediocrity rewarded to the white people around us. Addendums of the talk over time include what we don't learn about Black history in school, the horrors of slavery, details of the Black Panthers' work feeding Black students, or the race pride ideology of the Black women and men of the Harlem Renaissance. My parents included the other talk as part of their rotation of important lectures repeated during any lull in regular conversation. It wasn't until I understood enough about the concept of white supremacy that the words they spoke had true power for me.

What I didn't realize until—well, now—is the impact of those talks on my sense of belonging in those places—at school and at work. We tell Black girls that they have to work twice as hard and be twice as good as everyone else, but we don't explain how they'll be treated for actually being twice as good and working twice as hard as everyone else. It would've been almost impossible to explain that no amount of effort could buy my membership into the academy, as a minimal amount did for white students, or that the promise of success as a result of hard work wasn't the norm if you were Black. But there, at Vassar, shoulder to shoulder with students whose parents, grandparents, and maybe even generations before that belonged in this place, it was clear for whom this school was created. Their membership on campus was never in question, while I tried desperately to stake my claim and make my presence known.

Despite repeating the other talk many times, my parents didn't—and couldn't, really—warn me that existing in educational spaces would instill a sense of isolation that felt natural, as it was meant to, or that I would feel unwelcome in the spaces to which I've fairly earned entrance. They couldn't point to the pattern of suggestions that I don't look the part, that I'm not the "usual" Vassar girl, PhD candidate, or doctor because they were too proud of me to notice the toll my achievements took. They couldn't explain, in a way that would've made sense to my young brain, that insinuations that I just don't "look" the part of any of those roles—because of my braids or my age—are just code for Blackness. These coded messages that I don't belong in prestigious academic spaces are attempts to break me down via constant challenges to my belonging, but how can you know that until you experience it yourself?

The civil inattention to Blackness on campus, the process by which Black students are acknowledged but never fully engaged with as members of the campus culture, allows for the perpetual racing of Black students. We gravitate toward each other at HWSCUs because we share the same secret that our racial identity impacts everything that happens to us. Whether the white people around us believe that truth or not, connections that support the realities of being Black in white spaces are life-saving. Someone's dorm room, or a table in the dining hall, or just ninety minutes of time designated for the airing of grievances is relief from the nonstop pressure of being a Black student at a white school.

Credentialing

Higher education, and all of its components, establish racial order in ways that define the social and economic experiences of Black people. Schools, as physical manifestations of the institution of education, are where kids learn racism away from their families. As infants and toddlers, children rely on their parents and siblings to model interracial interactions, but the social consequences of those beliefs and behaviors are low at home. In school, racism is established as a system, a way of life, and is costlier to the victims than the perpetrators.

The process of establishing racism as systemic in school is incremental but absolute. First, the absence of Black students in gifted programs and advanced placement courses limits perceptions of our intellect. In 2012, Black students were less than 9 percent of students enrolled in gifted and talented programs in the US.[11] White students are twice as likely to be identified as gifted as Black students with the same standardized math and reading test scores.[12] Then, overrepresentation in detention and suspensions marks us as disobedient and potentially violent. As a result, Black students are four times as likely to be suspended as white students.[13]

Our skin color marks us as different, and implicit bias among teachers and administrators perpetuate the perceived role of Black students in school. Only 20 percent of Black K through 12 students were taught by the 4.4 percent of Black teachers in the United States in 2014. Black teachers are three times more likely to identify Black students as "gifted and talented," in part because they don't have the same negative preconceived notions about Black students belonging in school—notions developed long before they became teachers themselves. So, in the absence of Black teachers, the "racing" of Black students can happen unencumbered. By the time students get to college, these ideas have been instituted as a social fact. Black people on historically white-serving campuses are marked as trespassers, and are not only unwelcome but simply don't belong. I am exhausted by the work of standing out.

On campus, my Blackness marks me as anything other than a student or a teacher, a signal that I am perpetually mismatched with higher education. Black students, faculty, and administrators are all just as likely a part of the cleaning or dining hall staff in the minds of most white people on college campuses. I've been mistaken for cleaning or catering staff when I was a student *and* a faculty member. Ten years and three degrees later, I'm still just the Black woman who probably works here, serving the white people who actually belong.

Across the country, there are stories of Black people experiencing discrimination based on disbelief of their credentials. Aramis Ayala, a Florida state attorney, was pulled over by two police officers in Orlando in June 2017 after they ran her plates to check if the car was stolen.[14] In 2009, Harvard Professor Dr. Henry Louis Gates was arrested trying to enter his own home in the predominantly white neighborhood of Cambridge, Massachusetts, near the university.[15]

Over and over again, Black people report the need to assert educational attainment, professional credentials, and even class status to access and interact in the same spaces as white people. Accusations of a lack of credentials are derived from the same disbelief of Black academic success. How can we have advanced degrees, professional success, or economic stability if school is a place for them, not for us? We are rendered invisible because the perceived possibility that Black people are highly educated and successful is low. Yet because our presence is unexpected in college communities, we also stand out as trespassers in an institution responsible for maintaining our isolation from education and success.

This problem of credentialing always makes me think back on the lives of my great-grandmother, Alberta, and my grandmother, Leah. No pictures of graduations or diplomas were kept as honorifics to remember their success—only death certificates, yearbooks, and rumors to cement their histories. I didn't find out my grandmother Leah went to college and was a teacher until I was in college myself. The dissociation of Black kids and education allows for the perpetual challenging of our intellect and inability, but most white people are willfully ignorant of the ways in which school taught them what to expect Black people to *be*.

Black Silence

In 2016, after a talk I'd organized to bring a Black woman scholar to campus, a group of select faculty (myself included) got together with the guest lecturer for dinner. The topic of conversation turned to our students, as it so often does at these things, and we began taking turns sharing stories about students looking for grade changes at the end of our respective marking periods. The discussion was mostly congenial and lighthearted until a white woman professor shared a story about a Black woman student who came to her to advocate for a grade increase because of her desire to attend medical school.

According to this white woman, she responded to the student, "Stop stressing so much about a grade in one class," which alone would've been an appropriate response, but instead, she continued. "You don't have to worry about grades to get into medical school," she said. "You're a Black woman—of course you'll get in," she laughed.

To this day, I have no idea if this was an attempt at sarcasm revealing racial bias or just blatant, purposeful racism. This white woman's intention is irrelevant, though; it's a product of decades-long socialization into the very institution to which she belongs. Her willingness to say something so degrading to an anxious Black woman student, her boldness in enthusiastically retelling the story in a room full of Black women scholars, and her ignorance in thinking we'd laugh alongside her highlights the pervasiveness of the idea that Black academic success is merely mythological or political. She never stopped to think how we, Black women with advanced degrees, might feel hearing her equate our potential for achievement with affirmative action policies. Even now, I'm not sure that moment means anything to her other than an attempt to join the conversation, not important enough to recall easily.

For every Black woman in that room, though, it was another act of racist violence inflicted on us as punishment for occupying a space not meant for us. We called, texted, and emailed each other about this most recent attack on our being. I was especially ashamed and remorseful in our confabs about the presence of this woman at my event, the exposure of our guest to racism in what should have been a safe-*ish* space, and my failure to call out the blatant racism in the moment.

But then, none of us said anything. A handful of Black women PhDs sat at a dinner table and listened as a white woman told a racist joke at the expense of a Black woman student, and we said nothing. Our silence was, on one hand, tacit disapproval, but on the other hand, a result of decades of social training on how to exist as Black women in a historically white-serving space like this one. When those white spaces also offer high-status credentials, Black people often have to be willing to lose what we've worked for in exchange for direct confrontation with individual racism. The white folks around us are perfectly happy to let us explore institutional racism as long as we aren't calling out individuals. This white woman's joke was clearly racism, and we let it go.

Telling *this* "joke" among *this* group of Black women is the first offense here. The second is the message communicated to one of our Black students, and the danger (and audacity) of a faculty member who speaks to Black students this way. I wanted so badly to know the name of the student to whom she spoke if only to reassure her that it was racist nonsense. I remember being told over and over again as I achieved academically that my success was more about my race than my intellect, hard work, or even my privilege. I also remember how collectively devasting those comments were, the self-doubt they caused in me, and how starved I was for someone, especially a Black woman like me, to tell me that it was all bullshit.

I never found out who she was. To do so would have been to confront an institution that readily controlled me. I was still convinced that my entrance into academia would lead to increased social status and upward class mobility, which would neutralize a lot of the daily racism I've experienced. I wasn't yet disillusioned by my identity as a Black woman and the fixed social permanence of my degradation. I hadn't yet realized that my silence was a part of the performance of Blackness in the academy. Likewise, it was not the first time I'd been silent in the face of racism, just like that day twenty-five years ago with my face frozen in the snow.

5

The Performance of Belonging

In my senior year of college, I won the lottery. Unfortunately no actual money was involved, but instead something of both practical and social value: a desk. Not just a desk, but a dedicated desk in the hallows of the Vassar library, a library so beautiful and revered that it is known among both the local Poughkeepsie and Vassar communities as just The Library.* A desk among the most intellectual and hardworking of my peers. It seems silly to think about now, but every year a raffle was held that only senior students who were writing departmental theses could enter. Each of us put our name in the proverbial hat for a chance to be voluntarily chained to one of an exclusive set of 50-year-old hunks of wood for our entire senior

---

* Named after Frederick Ferris Thompson, a Vassar trustee and the husband of Mary Clark Thompson, who built the library and its extensions in 1918 and 1924 in memory of him.

year of college in the name of academic success. I never actually expected to be chosen, and I have no idea if this even still happens. It was just something else in the long line of somethings that I did to look the part. If the smartest and most successful students were all desperate for a desk, then I wanted to count myself among them.

These kinds of traditions at colleges and universities, those with histories and detailed narratives, tie individuals to the schools they attend via exclusive engagement. The most efficient way to belong in these environments is to gain membership to exclusive organizations, like Princeton's eating clubs, Ivy League secret societies, and even Vassar's Daisy Chain, on which I served as head daisy— all examples of the ways belonging at these prestigious schools is performed. Both public, and covert, the country's oldest and most prestigious institutions use these groups as campus gatekeepers separating the elite from the ordinary. For me, participation wasn't a guarantee, but a useful springboard to performing belonging.

That desk, and the subsequent eight months I spent voluntarily chained to it, were part of my performance of belonging at this school, in this major—sociology, with this work ethic. A vicious cycle of symbolic violence—the institution's way of redirecting unachieved success to internal blame among poor Black people, obscuring the roles that predetermined structures and culture play in our disadvantages—refocused my fears of worthiness inward, resulting in an uncertainty of my abilities, and hyper-awareness of my failures and the way they'd be perceived in predominantly white classrooms. So I spent hours in the library every day; it was the place to see and be seen working diligently. I pulled more books from the stacks than can be carried easily, out of fear that I'd lose the citation, and it didn't hurt for folks to see me overrun with information.

Thinking back on it, I don't remember many of my classmates actually caring about such things—they didn't have to. Their belonging is mapped in the whiteness, or their class membership, and most often their status as legacies. I had nothing to mark me as one of them; I didn't know much of the college's history. I never saw myself in the old photos of Vassar women hung in buildings across the college. Perhaps it was because there were so few Black women before 1970, but this was also evidence of a place, a college, not meant for me.

When I began writing my senior thesis in 2004, my anxiety and sense of non-belonging were at their apex. I was to write a fifty-page theoretical analysis on the topic of my choice. The task was to think sociologically, to show what I'd learned and make the jump from student to critical thinker—but I felt wholly inept. Not unprepared; a freshman year major declaration meant I'd had six full semesters of sociology courses and women's studies minor courses from which to draw, the only Black woman professor in the department as my thesis advisor and, most importantly, a dedicated desk in the library basement to write and store material. I didn't write for four months. Instead, I read, I met with my advisor when she had time, and I spent a shameful amount of time staring out the library's picture windows, but I couldn't put pen to page. I was paralyzed by my perceived incompatibility with this place, and the unlikeliness I'd actually finish.

Zora Neale Hurston's accounting of her own experiences as a Black woman at Barnard, another of the Seven Sisters colleges,[1] includes a description of the "stark white background" of the college, its classrooms, and social areas. Her words felt familiar to me even though I first read them more than ten years after graduating from Vassar College and seventy years after Hurston's experience. She unpacked, in far fewer words than I do here, what it means to feel like the Black hole in the place where you're supposed to be developing community, establishing bonds to the institution and its mission. What happens to those students for whom that natural belonging in higher education is impossible? How do we come to belong in those spaces? Hurston, as we sociologists are prone to do, doesn't offer solutions, only acknowledgments and descriptions of patterns of hyper-visibility and non-belonging for Black students.

Hurston calls herself the "sacred Black cow" of Barnard College, a description that still feels disappointingly accurate. As the institution's first Black graduate in 1928, she was exposed to an inherently disparate set of expectations on campus. It was not unexpected, because Barnard introduced Hurston with a small amount of fanfare, her race and background were known and prepared for in advance, before she transferred from Howard University. Yet she was still regarded as someone unfit to be a Barnard woman as-is. Instead, her style of dress, language use, and "manners" were all seen as inappropriate for the setting, and many of her white peers, even her friends, worked actively and consistently to "improve" her and thus improve her position on campus. Hurston was the center of attention and yet perpetually the odd man out, much like sacred cows wandering the streets of India, out of place in an industrial environment. She was welcomed as a symbol of goodwill and reference for Black exceptionalism, but ultimately seen as untoward when viewed through an American ethnocentric lens. Hurston died penniless in an unmarked grave. Alice Walker discovered her gravesite in Eatonville, Florida, in 1973. And in the 1980s, Zeta Phi Beta, the Divine Nine sorority in which Hurston was one of the first initiates while attending Howard University, made sure she was remembered and continued to help tell her story.

The Exhaustion of Fitting In

Hurston continued in part because of the value of Barnard's education to her after graduation, the main reason Black people develop performances to mimic ways of belonging not inherently available to us. The social capital of being a Vassar graduate was perhaps lost on me when I first applied and even when I was accepted. My college dreams included any scenarios where the average temperature was greater than sixty degrees and the opportunity to finally be my own person, far from what seemed then the confines of midwestern racism. I was looking for the opportunity to be among my peers, the other folks—Black, white, or other—who had trouble fitting in at high school. But like Hurston, when I arrived I found competition and ostracization among those I imagined I'd be embraced by.

That hurt was exactly what I felt as I sat helplessly on the floor of my dorm room next to the crumpled mess of fabric that was supposed to signal my belonging. It was my Daisy Chain dress, an ankle-length, white A-line dress with spaghetti straps that was special-ordered for all fifteen Daisies, sophomore women. It was supposed to be worn the following week during commencement exercises when the graduating seniors would walk through the literal chain of daisies resting on our shoulders.[2] But it didn't fit, probably because a fattening combination of dining hall food and depressive binge-drinking caused me to gain weight in all the wrong places. Beyond being embarrassing, this was disastrous for two reasons: (1) I was the head daisy and therefore (theoretically) "the leader," so looking unkempt in my dress would be a failure of leadership, and (2) I was the one Black person on the Daisy Chain, so if my dress didn't fit, there was no way to hide it. I would be front and center.

The pressure to be a "perfect Black" in these all-white settings, able to perform belonging that defies the stereotypical assumptions of the white people around us, is exhausting work. The pain of performance is physical, emotional, and psychological. The physical stress of stretching my lips over my teeth to force a smile after a racist remark, or biting my tongue in the face of a steady flow of racism and misogynoir so as not to be labeled aggressive or disagreeable has aged me just as much as the sadness, confusion, guilt, and anger at the requirement of such behavior, and the anxiety and depression that accompany them. I drank and smoked on campus to be social, but also to numb the constant anxiety of trying to fit in among people with whom I'd never fit under normal circumstances. As I lay in tears on my dorm room floor, next to my dress that was now too small, I felt the anxiety about my inability to perform my role as head daisy without the proper costume well up in my throat.

In his book *The Education of Black Folk*, Allen Ballard discusses what it was like for Stanley Jackson and him as the first two Black men enrolled at Kenyon College in 1948.[3] He recalls trying to manifest belonging within this predominantly white campus community, saying, "in retrospect, it is clear that—with some exceptions—our existence on that campus was defined not by us but by the constant necessity to be everything that negated the white man's concept of niggers."

This sentence, about experiences in 1948 and published in 1973, is an accurate description of my experiences in 2001 and the foundations of my research findings in 2018. After seventy years, college is still the place where Black students don't belong, and the performance of belonging means, as Ballard wrote, "[to be] forced to suppress our natural inner selves so as to conform to the mores of a campus dominated by upper middle class Americans. For eighteen hours a day, our manners, speech, style of walking were on trial before white America."

In this analogy, higher education for Black students isn't a sanctuary for learning and social and intellectual growth. It's a constant test, a place where movements, statements, dress, attitude, facial expressions, vocal inflections, and eye twitches can be reimagined into some slight against white people, a justification for racist assumptions about Black inferiority, or simply a reason for public ribbing. Ballard remembers, "classes, particularly in the freshman and sophomore years, although sometimes intellectually rewarding, seemed frequently to us, tests to prove to both teachers and students that Jefferson's views on the Black mentality were incorrect."

That day in middle-school science class, when I put myself and my intellectual curiosity on display only to be dismissed by my teacher and abandoned by my classmates, indicated the role classroom spaces play for Black students, or—more accurately—the role Black students must play in the classroom. This is especially true for those of us with dreams of attending prestigious institutions, accumulating academic accolades and exclusive group memberships, and participating in extracurricular activities that are necessities in the maintenance of belonging. It's also exhausting.

Exhaustion is the expected physical state among Black students trying to succeed in these settings. Our fatigue, though, is not considered debilitating; no one rushes to our aid when we collapse from overwork. Instead, we're questioned about why we're taking up space where we shouldn't be in the first place. It's an important feature of Black non-belonging where our overexertion and our suffering remain unnoticed in favor of that of our white peers.

My little sister and I share a private joke about the perpetual performance of belonging in school that imitates the infamous episode of *Saved by the Bell*—one of our favorite childhood Saturday morning shows—about Jesse Spano's drug addiction. We often act out her memorable monologue on the never-ending stressors of high school student life. We know how much all that costs, trying to be yourself in a world hell-bent on making you something else. So, when Jesse started screaming about all the things there's just no time to do, we couldn't help but nod in agreement.

The cheerleading team, track team, glee club, student council, full course load, and the boyfriend she's juggling in that "very special episode" were not far off from the impossible schedules I created for myself. The clubs, choirs, orchestras, sports teams, and leadership positions I went after in middle school, I had to keep up in high school and exceed in college. When my sister and I really get going, our voices dripping in sarcastic unison, we try to sound as sad and helpless as the white teen in this iconic scene while knowing full well that we'd never, and have never, been given the same opportunity to vent. We're never shown the same empathy in response to our overwork. So instead, we devolve into identical giggles at the irony of playing a role we'll never be offered. We laugh to keep from crying.

What We Do

The performance of belonging is not just about what you do to make it, it's also about what it costs you. The weight of Angela Davis's warning to critically examine the tools used to achieve success and the conditions under which victories are achieved in social movements is equally applicable in academia. In fact, the question of how we, those Black people who've accessed resources unavailable to the majority of Black communities, uncovered and then utilized such access—and to what ends—underlies the research questions in Michelle Obama's senior thesis. We've made it into these predominantly white spaces, we've learned the language of the intellectual, and developed a pattern of code-switching that allows us to move—somewhat—comfortably across cultures. But who must we become in exchange for these tools, for this access? What time is left to work out who we are? I find that I've spent so much time, especially at points in my life when the white students around me were finding themselves during college and graduate school, managing my belonging in the space, practicing an artificial belonging, that I'm just now beginning to explore myself, and shape my own self-concept. Before discussions of connections to academic achievement or professional success, belonging for Black women in academia often includes the suppression, especially during our formative years, of our authentic selves.

The performance of belonging in academic spaces for Black women, then, is more complex than mere assimilation. Honestly, it sounds easier to adopt completely the culture of the ruling class than to exist as a dual-citizen among the rulers but of the ruled. We are constantly hyper-visible at these HWSCUs, but our visibility doesn't protect us from harm or degradation within their walls. In fact, many Black students come to expect exposure to social, psychological, and physical harm so often that we barely recognize the racism in our everyday interactions at the actual volume we experience it. At Vassar, there were few spots for Black students and forty years of unattended complaints to solidify a perception of non-belonging and imply disinterest in directly addressing racism in the campus community.

A 2019 incident at fellow Seven Sister Barnard College saw the physical and verbal assault of a Black student by campus safety officers regarding his right to be in the library,[4] a glaring example of perpetual non-belonging at HWSCUs and the resulting traumatization of constant threats to personal safety simply because he was Black on campus. This Black student had to prove his belonging to gain entrance into a library to which access is a part of his tuition. Vassar's campus safety officers, too, have been accused of profiling and antagonizing Black students and faculty who don't appear to "belong" on campus. This is what it means to be Black on a white campus. You'll never truly belong, so your safety is always in jeopardy.

In 1977, a group of Black women students at Vassar put together a prospective student pamphlet called "At Vassar," specifically written for Black prospective students. In a lot of ways, the pamphlet—much like this book—was meant to be a collection of information and experiences from Black women for Black students. The pamphlet was no longer being circulated by the time I applied for college (I discovered it in the school's special collections decades later), and yet I had to undertake the same negotiation of self that was necessary for survival on campus twenty-four years before I arrived. The pamphlet warned of the "unfavorable effects" of attending a school where 80 percent of students are white, and rather than offering the same narrative as the college and so many other HWSCUs—that inclusion and diversity are celebrated, and Black students feel wholly welcomed and included into the campus community—it offered sobering realities of the difficulties of being Black on a campus where it feels like everyone else is white. They warn, "at times you will experience a dilemma in your efforts to avoid losing touch with yourself, your peers, your culture, and your ideals. A balance must be maintained between your past experiences and your new circumstances. If you can incorporate these two worlds, Vassar can provide the academic and social challenges which foster growth and strength."

The student writers were clearly dealing with the weight of performing belonging in this setting and trying to lessen the blow for the Black students who follow them. It makes me sad and angry to read, but it also feels so familiar, and I'm therefore relieved to know my negative experiences on campus weren't exclusively my fault, that they weren't a reflection of my own personal failings and shortcomings, but rather assumed and built into the very fabric of the institution with lasting effect, and shared with a long line of Black women alumni on these predominantly white campuses.

The complex duality we negotiate is founded on the very double-consciousness lamented by Du Bois over one hundred years ago—a requirement of Black people to segment their racial identity from other, less polarizing identities when engaging with white people—and demands the use of self-preservation mechanisms to survive. I needed a way to preserve some of myself without sacrificing my accumulated social and cultural capital or risking my potential for upward social mobility. I needed a mask, and I needed a routine. The traditional scripts, costumes, and staging for the performance of "student" or "professor" can't work for Black women because they are both developed with expectations of whiteness. When I walk into a classroom, as a student or as a professor, my intelligence and accomplishments are not assumed. Those characteristics that *are* assumed of me have little connection to education.

My performance in the classroom is a response to stereotypes, attempts to disarm my Blackness in predominantly white settings, and involves an intricate combination of scripts and costumes designed to defuse the audience and neutralize the negative impact of race and subsequent behavioral expectations. White students and administrators, largely in control of my experiences at school, respond positively to interactions with those Black folks who perform these scripts, which allows for willful ignorance of the professor's racial identity. I knew that. I learned it early, and I engaged in it often—still do—when the settings necessitate, but to engage in this type of face work is arduous, often debilitating labor.

How We Do It

When I was eighteen years old, a first-semester freshman, I was introduced to the social theorist Erving Goffman and it changed my life. "Dramaturgy is the theory of all social life as theater, and therefore executed theatrically in social interactions," my sociology professor began as part of the morning lecture on Erving Goffman.

I'd spent the weekend devouring *Presentation of Self in Everyday Life*,[5] the assigned reading for the week, and though the book doesn't grapple with race directly I felt goosebumps as his words described things I'd experienced but never before had the language to discuss. It was like learning a language I'd heard all my life. I declared as a sociology major the next day. The sociological theory of life as theater felt familiar and true to life because, in many ways, anytime I wasn't at home with my family, anytime I was with my white friends, in my schools, or at my white jobs with my white coworkers, I was acting. I was playing the part of an inoffensive Black person in order to belong where white people would rather I did not.

When I interviewed other Black professional women for my dissertation research on career trajectories in a predominantly white city, the women all discussed the performances they engaged in, effectively under duress, to maintain and improve their financial and professional opportunities.[6] Those who chose not to perform in this way, intentionally opting out of "the game," reported lower salaries, subordinate job titles, and less autonomy in the workplace than those who discussed the mechanisms of their professional performance as integral to their daily survival. In the end, we're all losers. We can lose pieces of ourselves, stunt the growth of our self-concept, and have a chance at a semblance of success, or try to remain authentic to the cultures in which we were raised and risk access to the most effective and efficient roads to upward social mobility.

So, we have to "front." Or perhaps I should just speak for myself: I front. I use whiteface performance, code-switching, and cultural flexibility to move through spaces that'd otherwise be denied to me. Erving Goffman's concept of "front," "that part of the individual's performance which regularly functions in a general and fixed fashion to define the situation for those who observe the performance" (p. 22),[7] is usually more scenic in form, describing the setting in which said interaction takes place, the dress of the actors. The structure of the interaction takes center stage. But "front" for Black women in educational spaces is more a verb than a noun. Because Black students are never inherently expected in educational settings, we constantly front to assuage white fear of our unexpected presence there.

Our fronts are mechanisms to ensure, as much as any Black person is able, our safety and protect our continued admittance into these spaces. Because we are not *supposed* to be proactively entering learning spaces, it's impossible to be authentic and acceptable. In his theory of social performance, Goffman argues, "if an individual is to give expression to ideal standards during [her] performance, then [she] will have to forgo or conceal action which is inconsistent with these standards" (p. 41). As both Black and woman, Black women are uniquely inconsistent with ideal standards for "student" or "professor." Our actions are perceived as innately unsuitable for education, an ideology with violent ends, especially in predominantly white schools where structural and cultural racism go unchecked by all-white administrations and Black students have little recourse for advocacy on their behalf.

Our performance of the educated, cultured Negro has long been one of entertainment for white people. Enslaved people were rarely educated, but those who were taught to read and write by white slave owners discovered that their teachers were sympathizers interested in parading an educated slave as a novelty, or often to soothe their own loneliness by creating a "worthy" companion.[8]

The willingness to continue these performances in perpetuity is, for most of us, not because we enjoy pretending to be someone else. I wouldn't describe what I do in the classroom, either as a teacher or student, as pretending to be something I'm not. Likewise, I have no interest in blanket assimilation into white culture. But because I don't feel safe in predominantly white spaces, and good performances increase the likelihood of my safety—and maybe even my success, where it was otherwise inherently insecure—I perform the role of an "acceptable" Black person. My life as a Black person in white spaces means moving in ways that make white people feel comfortable, regardless of my personal comfort level. The emotional and physical strength required to manage that kind of psychological and spiritual duality drains my ability to handle the everyday stressors of being a human in the world.

The Non-Threatening Black Friend

My hair, now a full, soft mass of chin-length kinky curls, was the most difficult part of my performance to control. The bald spots on the edges of my hairline at twenty-three years old served as evidence of the price of making my "unruly" hair "tame"; a part of the attempted performance for Black girls at HWSCUs. I wore microbraids almost continuously from eighth grade through graduate school because it was easier to protect my natural hair from inquisitive and often outright racist white peers and limited the amount of manipulation necessary for a Black girl athlete like me. It didn't help that I've lived and worked in predominantly white areas all my life; places where access to the proper products for Black hair care is never promised.

Black hair has long been a source of discrimination against Black people. In 2019, California Governor Gavin Newsom signed the Crown Act into state law, legally protecting hairstyles against explicit discrimination in work and school settings. The idea that our kinky-curly locks are inappropriate for "professional" settings like work and school also perpetuates the idea that we don't belong there, and Black hairstyles are discriminated against in public settings with little recourse. Braids made the performance of belonging at school, sleepovers with white friends, and living with white roommates less socially awkward, but my hair paid the price. In 2012 my hair was so unhealthy that I had to cut it all off and start over.

Comedian and actress Amanda Seales tells a great joke about identifying Black girls who grew up as the only Black girl in a group of white girls. We know all the words to Wilson Phillips's "Hold On," she jokes, implying that memorizing it was a requirement for entrance into white teen communities in the 1990s, and she's right. I am one of those Black girls; I had to be aware of music I wouldn't be exposed to via my parents, older cousins, or other family members in order to belong in my group of white friends. Being able to belt out "someday somebody's gonna make you want to turn around and say goodbye," on cue and in perfect unison and harmony, was one of many litmus tests for belonging among my white girlfriends.

Later it was staying caught up on the latest episode of *Dawson's Creek* and shopping at Abercrombie & Fitch—even though the clothes are clearly not for larger, curvy bodies like mine—that signaled my membership in groups of white teens. The kids we go to school with, and the school itself, police the sustainability of our public performances of belonging. Knowing the words and being able to sing along in group karaoke sessions was a prerequisite to belonging with my white classmates, just one example of a multitude. These were the scripts, costumes, and stages of Goffman's dramaturgy. I was acting a part to belong where I didn't, where many people thought I shouldn't, and that performance was the currency I used to gain entrance and maintain access to spaces where Black people are often shut out.

The impact of these performances, both on my internal self-concept and professional successes, was just as split as the performances themselves. I wanted to belong, and being able to perform belonging via shared experiences and language use with the overwhelming number of white people I interact with in academia afforded me at least minimal access to that feeling. A sense of perceived belonging in school is correlated with grade point average, class participation, and graduation rate. In historically white-serving settings, my performances were attached to my successes in ways for which I did not yet have words. I understood innately what was being asked of me, and am (still) acutely able to read situations and adjust my performances for optimum acceptance in predominantly white settings. As I write this, I'm aware of how maladjusted these musings on performance must make me sound, but the truth is, there is a permanent sense of flux for Black people who spend the majority of their time in predominantly white settings.

One of the underlying assumptions of Goffman's theory of dramaturgy is that people engage in social performances to make some part of themselves significant to others. We stand to gain from the quality and appropriateness of our performances in social interactions, so we continually engage in them, practicing and perfecting these performances in perpetuity. But to perform constantly is an exhausting endeavor. Goffman rarely engages with the ways some performances impact our mental and physical health. However, there is evidence in the shorter life spans and predisposition to heart disease, stroke, and other stress-related ailments with no genetic foundation that are seemingly endemic to Black communities. Instead, he frames interaction through performance as a thing that happens when the actors, for various reasons, are committed to the engagement and its potential for positive impact. Black people moving through white spaces don't have the same power to pick and choose performances in this way, instead our performances and all their associated requirements are predetermined. If Black people are social actors engaged in theater, then we perform back-to-back-to-back shows on a loop, with few spaces where we can actually safely and securely be ourselves. Our backstage, the place where we are free from acting, is never guaranteed.

To Talk "Right"

"I ain't do nothing to him," I explained to my mom on our car ride home from the airport. "Did you say 'ain't'?" she responded, ignoring my statement and focusing squarely on my sentence construction rather than the details of the story being retold. I was fourteen years old and returning home from eight weeks with my extended family in Milwaukee. This reminder of how I *should* speak was an annual dance we did as I recalibrated from a summer surrounded by my all-Black family and life in the predominantly white world to which I was returning. "No," I answered sullenly. Instead of revising my words to the Standard English "didn't" as I knew she wanted, I just stopped talking. These mini-linguistics lessons I knew were meant to perfect my speech at school. However, the constant correction was frustrating to me as a new teenager, still learning how to express my feelings in general, let alone having to shape them via a dialect with which I didn't always feel comfortable.

Language is the primary and most policed part of the performance of belonging for Black people in school. Language reflexivity, the ability to switch seamlessly between dialects, cultural cues, and language settings with ease, is not innate. Like language acquisition in children, earlier exposure, immersion, and practice are required to develop a fluent skill set. As a little Black girl in predominantly white schools, I had plenty of time and opportunity to acquire and practice perfecting this craft, and my mother made sure I practiced whenever possible. It also created a well of social anxiety that is difficult to quell. I continued because the benefits of perfect performances are as clear to me as the penalties of a poor one. I've developed a kind of PTSD, I'm sure shared by other Black students educated in predominantly white schools. As a result, I can recoil and invert at the thought of social interactions in predominantly white settings. It became important to seek out or manifest for myself a few spaces to allow for some stolen moments to express my extroverted nature that is mischaracterized as stereotypically loud and aggressive coming from a Black woman.

This language reflexivity is not something Black people *choose* to learn. We can choose when and where to utilize specific performances, especially if we're ambivalent about the social consequences, but never have we had the right to maintain interaction in African American English Vernacular (AAEV) in predominantly white settings. Jamaican philosopher Charles Mills's racial contract theory argues that the tacit agreement among all social actors promotes and maintains white supremacy and demands language reflexivity of Black people in exchange for the *chance of* professional success.[9] His interactional theory breaks down racism at the center of interactions between social actors.

The racial contract not only encourages our performances with promises of rewards but it also forces them through threats of violence. On predominantly white college campuses, increased racist hate crimes highlight modern-day manifestations of the racial contract. Amherst College, American University, Duke University, and the University of South Alabama are just a few college campuses where nooses were found hanging from trees on campus in recent years,[10] continuing the history of white students terrorizing Black students at school. At my own institution, groups of white students

carrying Trump signs and American flags taunted students protesting President Trump's election win with chants of "build the
wall" in full view of faculty, administrators, and fellow students,
events that precipitated my resignation from the diversity committee. There was no sense of empathy for students of color fearful
of political persecution. In fact, these students were attempting to
assert the white supremacy of the institution, believing it their right
to do so. The fact that they are not required to demonstrate decorum on campus the way Black students are means that very little
of white students' behavior is out of bounds. White students must
be understood, or at least empathized with, rather than disciplined
because of assumptions of deviance as Black students are. These
are the same students whom many conservative politicians deem to
be too young and too innocent to learn about "divisive" concepts
like racism and white supremacy. So much energy is exerted to make
sure white students feel supported and protected—Black students
be damned.

Those students' words are devoid of any superficial performance
of belonging. For them, belonging in this historically white-serving
space is inherent. They can insinuate unwelcomeness and intimate
potential violence without worrying about their own continued
acceptance in the place, while the students they threaten—the ones
protesting for equality—are the ones singled out as instigators of
unrest, threats to the status quo. It is not a coincidence that some
of the same nasty tactics used by white people trying to prevent
desegregation in the 1950s are used by white students today. The
distaste for Black kids is ongoing. White folks who were photo-
graphed yelling obscenities at Black students during integration
are still alive today. This is another reason to avoid teaching the
historical foundations of racism in schools—to make those tactics
feel removed from the present, relics of a distant past and divorced

from the current moment. It's better than seeing your picture in a textbook.

I thought things would work differently once I finished my PhD; then, as I struggled for attention on the tenure-track job market, I thought a tenure-track job would be where I would find equality among other academics, those who'd also successfully persevered in and triumphed over their own PhD programs. But instead, I found the need for never-ending performances. There is a depressive truth in that fact, that even the highest degree couldn't prevent the necessity for a constant reinforcement of my qualifications to maintain access to academic spaces. I still have to dance and jig to maintain my position, maintain my minute financial stability, and maintain my credibility among my students and coworkers.

Belonging in Sociology

Operation Varsity Blues, the 2019 fraud scandal implicating wealthy white parents trying to purchase their children's admission at some of the country's most prestigious colleges and universities, reminds us that assumptions of belonging in higher education are mapped on to race. These white students didn't have to perform the hard work and perseverance required of Black students trying to make their case for entrance into the same schools. Belonging is an innate feature of whiteness, unchanged even as the potential students themselves are uninterested in the work of college attendance. Black students, on the other hand, are required to engage in exhausting performance to *potentially* access the same degree, but that too is misrepresented as "robbing" white applicants of potential spots that Black overachievers are "hogging."

News anchors unapologetically and non-ironically criticize the small percentage of Black students receiving a dozen offers from the country's most prestigious schools because their viewers, white or Black, have long come to understand white students as "belonging" in college and Black students as making it there via diversity and inclusion policies.[11] This happens long before we ever think about going to college, and it's reinforced when white kids, but not Black ones, see themselves depicted as college students on TV, in film, and among family members with college degrees. For white kids, then, education feels inheritable—even if class membership means their actual access to college may be minimal, a rite of passage guaranteed to them as it has been for their parents and grandparents before them. By contrast, Black people have continued difficulty locating themselves in the culture and history of higher education. Visits to archives at my alma mater institutions, as I tried to understand what, if any, legacy my education stems from, reminded me of our invisibility in the history of higher education. We were there, but our contributions remain buried and mostly undocumented over time.

As an undergraduate, I never found an opportunity to focus on the social construction of race as my raison d'être for majoring in sociology, even as I overloaded on classes with the only Black professor in the department—one of a handful at the school—who also taught race-focused courses in the department. I did not only find it difficult to belong on campus as a sociology major, but I also found little space—outside Dr. Harriford's classes—for discussions of race, and even in graduate school saw race relegated to the sidelines as another in a cluster of independent variables probably impacting the more important dependent variables under study.

I was thirty years old before I learned exactly how much Du Bois influenced modern sociology, specifically in the empirical study of race. I believed the mostly white sociologists who trained me and encouraged my focus squarely with white theorists, many dubbed the "founding fathers" of sociology. It limited my view of race-based research as legitimate and worthwhile, and guided me away from what is now the center of my research and teaching focus. The road back to race research has been long, arduous, and lonely. Before I would become the same lone Black woman in a sociology department half the size of Vassar's, Dr. Harriford was the only Black sociologist with whom I'd have contact until I was well through my doctoral program.

I took every course on race offered in my department and any tangential departments where I had the prerequisites. However, I was still mostly taught by white professors, filled with discussions dominated by white students, and assigned readings by mostly white researchers. I felt consistently pushed away from race as the focus of my undergraduate study and instead wrote my senior thesis on the spectrum of sexual attraction. The topic, though interesting to me personally, is not the story I wanted to tell.

What I realize now as a professor who does just that—focuses on race and racism—is the impact on Black peoples' lives and the legitimacy of "race research" as a matter of import in theoretical approaches to teaching and scientific investigations in the discipline. Identifying myself as an investigator of institutional racism reduces perceptions of my work as personal and nonscientific. It leaves me open to criticism and opinion from students, fellow faculty, and administrators. I am forced into performances not required of my white colleagues by virtue of the relationship between my race and my research focus. This is in part because whiteness continues to frame academic hierarchies—especially across older disciplines. Without me, the department would be entirely white and devoid of discussions of racism not derived from the white gaze. In fact, before me, no Black woman lasted more than three years in the department. None was awarded tenure. This is not a coincidence.

Whiteness continues to frame academic structures, perverting and sometimes completely erasing Black contributions to the academy. In reality, a strong argument can be made, most eloquently by Dr. Earl Wright II at University of Cincinnati, that Black sociologists are the backbone of sociological thought.[12] For example, Anna Johnson Julian, the first Black woman in the United States to earn a PhD in sociology, did so from the University of Pennsylvania in 1937.[13] Julian would go on, with her husband, to establish Julian Laboratories, a company specializing in synthesizing hormones in bulk. However, her teaching options were limited to HBCUs, where the majority of Black sociologists would be siloed for the next fifty years. I wasn't introduced to Dr. Julian's research on childhood education until graduate school, and even then, I discovered her by accident. Not unlike Mary Terrell, who'd go on to teach at Dunbar High School, and E. Franklin Frazier and Charles S. Johnson, both from the University of Chicago School of Sociology,[14] I'd discovered the rich work on the social analysis of Black experiences from Black sociologists which was ignored by "mainstream" white sociologists for almost one hundred years, even though their work uncovers important information about the human condition.

Though I did not hear her name until I'd been embedded in the discipline for at least ten years, I quickly identified with Julian's plight. She was mostly turned away from faculty work at non-HBCUs, where competition for positions was steep. Her contributions as a trailblazer are overlooked, limiting the number of Black women following in her footsteps, disconnected from the legacy of valued intellectual thought in the history of sociology. That Julian, Du Bois, Hurston, Frazier, or the many other Black sociologists who heavily contributed to the formation of American sociology as we know it remain so obscure whitewashes the entire discipline. And really, that is the point. Eliminating their contributions defines who sociologists are and what scientific study in sociology looks like. I never imagined myself as a sociologist, even as a sociology graduate student. I still felt myself trying to break into a science wholly foreign to me until I went in search of my own knowledge rather than expecting to be introduced to the knowledge I sought.

Not everyone is willing to endure the physical and psychological trauma of performing in predominantly white academic spaces, though. Ms. (Walls) Lanier withstood the masses of white racists who greeted the Little Rock Nine every morning on their way to school. Then, she and her Black classmates endured daily physical and mental abuse from white students in hallways, bathrooms, and the lunchroom. But not all of the Little Rock Nine were willing or able to take on that trauma voluntarily. Two students, Elizabeth Eckford and Minnijean Brown, completed high school via correspondence, withdrawing from public schooling completely to revoke white people's physical access to their lives. It was a reasonable choice for these Black women who, while prepared for verbal vitriol, were not willing to endure the physical harassment waiting for them at school for another year. That is a fact of belonging in predominantly white spaces: It isn't just about the social or psychological; it is steeped in the physical.

6

Body Work

I remember waking up, but not making a sound. It's the only time I can remember, now or then, when I woke without opening my eyes. That's usually a reflex for me, but this night I didn't. Perhaps it was my version of fight or flight, that concept of what we do as humans when we sense danger. The truth is, though, we never know how we'll respond until we're in that moment, and up until then—when I awoke to feel the unwelcome hands of a man I thought was my friend on parts of my body he'd never been given permission to explore—I thought for sure that I'd fight, risking physical harm over sexual assault, but I didn't fight; I didn't run. I had just lain there, trying to play dead until it was over.

I didn't want this, what was happening to me, but it wasn't completely surprising. It was only November of my freshman year, but since I'd arrived at Vassar several white men (though not only them) crossed physical boundaries I'd previously assumed were implied.

I'd also had several conversations with other women of color who'd relayed similar experiences of white men on campus touching them and speaking to them in ways that were overtly sexually suggestive, and not always welcome. We'd commiserated on the likelihood of constant fetishization by our white male peers and the insecurity that was imbued in our interactions with them.

If high school is where Black students perfect general performances of belonging, then college—this unique combination of living and work space, devoid of consistent "adult" supervision and that encourages participation in hookup culture—is where performances are situated in the physical body most. It's not enough to manage language reflexivity, memorize scripts, or perfect costumes; your body becomes a more specific and important focus at HWSCUs for sexual exploitation and physical discipline. Black women are in danger there. I thought I'd act violently, aggressively forcing my attacker to rethink his assault, but in the moment I played dead without consciously considering the consequences of a more assertive response. Perhaps I played dead because that had become my go-to move anytime I'd been victimized in learning spaces. I had learned to use passivity, especially bodily passivity, to avoid danger in this institution.

When conceptualizing this book, I knew I wanted to explore the physiological impacts of continued existence in predominantly white learning spaces because so many of my own experiences have been rooted in my physical presence. My visceral responses to performing belonging, the misuse and mistreatment of my body in predominantly white public spaces, and the focus on the acceptability of my body and its adornments in predominantly white classrooms are all issues I dealt with as a Black student at HWSCUs, and deal with still as faculty in those same spaces. These issues may not have started in the classroom, but they were certainly exacerbated there.

Black women are biologically seven-and-a-half years older than white women.[1] Our bodies are physically taxed by perpetual experiences of racism and misogynoir in our daily lives. The racial battle fatigue we experience is literally shortening our lives—of course we struggle in our bodies. I have an uneasy relationship with my body that started long before my sexual assault. She always knows when I'm overanxious about a looming deadline or apprehensive about a relationship. It's a feature I really hate. Sometimes my protector and keeper of secrets, others an arch-enemy seemingly focused on destroying me, my body is a constant reflection of the supremacist structures policing it. Like so many Black women's bodies, this one has been discussed, critiqued, and sometimes obsessed over ad nauseum. The perpetual state of surveillance in which Black women persist seeks to stifle the physical emancipation from white supremacist control over our bodies. We are always in danger of being yanked back into the spotlight, and it's hard to grow comfortable in a body like that.

The hyper-surveillance of my body began in school, and as a result, physiological manifestations of stress, fear, and anxiety about how my body was regarded began in school as well. Black students are more likely to be arrested in school than their white peers, though there are no statistics that show they actually misbehave more often. Institutional discipline for Black students is routinely harsher and a result of subjective infractions compared to white students. Black girls are one-and-a-half times as likely to be arrested at school than white girls, and Black boys are three times as likely as white boys.[2]

It started, as it does for most women despite their race, when I was going through puberty. I grew more than seven inches in what felt like a matter of weeks, which left me feeling big, exposed, and uncontrolled in a family filled with short, small women. It didn't help that this growth spurt corresponded with—or maybe was the catalyst for—an onset of anxiety that intensified in public spaces, especially at school. It was at school where my body was suddenly being policed.

My infractions were usually small and benign relative to those that my white classmates bragged about getting away with, but it was often I who ended up doing my homework in an empty classroom for detention after school. There was one white male teacher in particular who seemed to get joy out of making me seem insolent. "Are you chewing gum?" he asked during eighth-grade wood tech one winter afternoon. I froze, knowing that even though there were at least three other girls at my table who were also chewing gum—one of whom provided it to the rest of us before the first bell—I was about to bear the brunt of this infraction. "Oh, yeah, sorry," I replied. "I forgot to spit it out before class started."

I knew from experience that trying to point out others who were also guilty would do nothing but agitate him. He wasn't interested in what the white students were doing, despite the fact that their behavior often threatened our safety around all of the machines in the class "shop."

"Do you know why we don't chew gum in here?" the teacher asked non-ironically. Not waiting for my answer, he continued, "Because gum in the wrong place can ruin these expensive machines. You probably don't realize it, but they're worth quite a bit of money. Come get your detention slip," he added, as I almost imperceptibly shook my head and made my way to his desk to receive my sentence. Detention was more socially embarrassing than anything else. My mom worked so much that coming home from school a few hours late would go unnoticed as long as my homework was done, and I was still getting an A in the class. But being singled out made me fodder for mocking among classmates and tainted my performance of belonging among my all-white teachers.

In school, Black women's bodies have been hyper-sexualized and over-disciplined since integration, with continued stories of brutality across the last seventy years. I was twelve years old but suddenly being targeted as a potential siren, capable of distracting the men around me and luring them into my own abuse. My skirts and shorts were suddenly too short for sitting in class leading to consistent length checks of my clothing by mostly white administrators. They never accosted my white girlfriends in the same way, despite the similarities in our clothes. Instead, I was reminded there was something about my body that was different, that attracted different energy, and elicited different responses. It changed me.

Black women's bodies have been hyper-sexualized and viewed as entertainment for others since our enslavement. Saartjie Baartman is the most well-known example of the objectification and public exploitation of the Black body.[3] The Black South African woman's diminutive stature (she was four feet, ten inches) and extraordinarily curvy shape made her a profitable draw for white people obsessed with her body. Pejoratively known as the Hottentot Venus, Baartman was exhibited across Europe, displayed as an oddity; her body's "peculiarities" were used as evidence of Baartman's—and thus all Black people's—distance from whiteness. Baartman's objectification is the oldest but far from the only example of Black women's reduction to bodies in public discourse. Serena Williams's muscle structure, Megan Markle's skin color, and Beyoncé's body shape are all topics of conversation in public media accustomed to critiquing our very existence.

On college campuses, issues of sexual assault, rape, and harassment are framed via the experiences of white women, but Black women are more likely to be assaulted at school. In fact, recent research at Duke University estimates that approximately 42 percent of Black women had experienced some kind of sexual assault.[4] As Vassar, I was subject to not just that singular episode of sexual assault but a handful of other attempts, a constant barrage of sexually suggestive language masked as jokes, and a hyper-focus on my body that led to a severe bout of generalized anxiety order that I'm still being treated for today, all before my twentieth birthday. Middle school and high school were where I learned that my body was a thing to be disciplined; in college, expectations of sexual availability were added as additional layers of humiliation and degradation.

I've spent an inordinate number of hours, days, even months at a time thinking about my body. Not just the typical internal administrative checklist of physical and mental health: *Are my muscles tense? Do I have a stomachache? Am I hungry?* We all work our way through these checklists each day, creating smaller sub-lists for the never-ending diversity of tasks in need of completion. As a Black woman, I've developed an alternative set of observations learned after decades of walking this body into the predominantly white educational settings I frequent: *Did I sound too aggressive? Was I too loud, too forward, or too prepared? Am I taking up too much space, too much time? Am I too available, or too arrogant?* My understanding of how I fit into place as a Black woman has almost always been in conjunction with my body. These questions arise from the fundamental understanding of my body, constantly in need of restriction and constraint for acceptance.

The concentration on our bodies often starts at home, but also extends out into all of our social experiences. Before I really understood how and why my body had changed, it became the focus of conversation and critique—from me, my family, and friends, but also from strangers on the street. Perhaps I'd relate to my body more positively if I was able to grow into it and get to know its intricacies, before being subject to the scrutiny of second-class citizenry, but as a Black woman, I was never afforded the time for self-discovery.

Who Can I Trust, if I Can't Trust Myself?

Growing up as a Black girl and coming to understand what I, in this body, signal to others is a lesson I wish I'd learned *before* my body became part of public discussion. Being made aware of this dissection of my physical form by others before I ever really consciously inhabited it myself spawned animosity in me, toward everyone with specific remarks about my body, and toward my body itself for the betrayal of attracting so much attention. From the moment I entered puberty, I was constantly reminded of its inconvenience. I felt ambushed, forced to live a life in a body before I was completely aware of its rapidly changing consequences, and forced to distinguish my body from my identity rather than having the opportunity to grow as a whole person. I felt betrayed by this thing—my body, with which I was inextricably linked. It makes sense, then, that I took my frustrations with the plague of constant surveillance out on my arms and legs, on my skin, with whatever sharp edges I could find, as punishment for daring to exist at all.

Black women are taught to mistrust our bodies long before we reach puberty. My dad started repeating the old father-daughter mantra that men only wanted me for sex well before my 13th birthday. On car rides, he'd annoyingly list all the ways he could prove that what he was saying was fact as I sat in exasperated silence. At family gatherings, my dad would call me from across the room to recite those sex lessons. I found the entire process tiring and embarrassing, which was at least part of the point: to wear me down into submission until I was too annoyed or too afraid to have sex.

This process was the opposite of body positivity. The instillation of ideas about men's intentions was intended to erode my trust in others, especially men, to prevent my "dumb" decisions. In this narrative, I, and all "good" women, are positioned as perpetual potential victims of the uncontrollable sex drives of men. When it came to my body, I was to trust no one, including myself.

My body betrayed me by transforming from a prepubescent child to a thirteen-year-old, five-foot-seven-inch "developed" teen overnight. In comparison to the still preteen boys around me, I was big, suddenly both dangerous and enticing. Family and strangers alike, wondered aloud in amazement how I could be so big when my mother was so small, and I had to learn quickly that my body often arrived in a crowded room before I ever did. I now understand how the comments on my clothes, tattoos, muscle tone, or hairstyle, leveled at me like hand grenades, were the litmus test for my suitability in a particular setting. If I reacted too aggressively, I risked marking my body as incompatible with whatever predominantly white space in which this happened, because it always happened in predominantly white spaces. But if I reacted too passively, I opened my body to potential abuse and degradation at the hands of white supremacy.

As my body developed, and I tried to understand the quick and shocking changes, every comment was a new police-issued flashlight on this body in which I was trying to make myself at home. Designed to blind me so others could stare at and explore my body without interruption, the comments were disorienting and many times caught me off guard when I thought them honest reflections of some necessary external deficiencies. My body was too often at the forefront of discussion for my taste, so I set out to make it more acceptable. I attempted to blend in, thinking that if I was just as skinny as the popular white girls at school, on television, and in magazines, or if my style was just trendy enough, my speech unaffected, or my volume quiet enough, that I'd fade seamlessly away from the spotlight and be left in peace to learn, and later to teach and write. Fading from the spotlight is rarely an option for Black women, as I would come to learn, because the thing about the Black woman's body is that it's always the center of attention in a room, even when it's not.

The Art of Body Management

When you inhabit a hyper-visible and branded body as I do, you learn to micromanage the inherent stigma of being a Black woman. Learning that the successful management of our bodies in public settings can be life or death leads many Black women to memorize and constantly evaluate the checklist of intricate performances with which our bodies are tasked. It also encourages us to refer to ourselves in the third person—bodies, devoid from ourselves.

Body management of Black people is one of many lasting vestiges of slavery. The enslaved who were assigned house duties were often subject to additional hygiene rituals not required of field slaves, in part increasing their proximity to whiteness. Post-emancipation, presenting oneself as clean and well-kept was perceived as one of the few routes to assimilation. My aunties—raised on deep southern ideology despite migrating north to escape Jim Crow's terrorism before they were old enough to remember—never missed an opportunity to lament the waiting horror should any of their Black nieces smell unscented or look un-kept in public settings. To hear them tell it, the resulting embarrassment and isolation would be too much to bear.

Perceptions of Black women's bodies are at the center of this conflict. Constructed by whiteness as excessive so as to naturally position and limit all that which our bodies *do,* we have to fight off such constraints just to survive. We can't be too loud, too sexual, too strong, too fat, too inquisitive, or too fierce without fear for our personal safety. We are perpetually unfamiliar, and our bodies—a referendum on white morality—act as a literal wall between Black women and true belonging to any dominant social community.

Even at school, where our bodies are engaged in spectacle constantly, I found myself the Black dot in a sea of white ones, a body that physically and socially stands out. Whether during track or rugby practice (back when I was younger and much more limber), in the gym weight lifting (and minding my business), or during my weekly hot yoga and adult ballet classes, I am one of a few Black people and there my body becomes a public commodity on which others are free to appraise and comment. I cannot outrun or reposition my broad shoulders or the muscle tone in my arms and the heaviness of my thighs. They're all there, all the pieces of my body being figuratively taken apart—judged. Each piece was carefully considered for its potential to exert power where I, a Black woman, should have none.

My body means something in ways I'm still struggling to understand. Men, white and Black, find the breadth of my shoulders menacing, so it didn't take long for this little Black girl to realize I was different. I am different. Being a Black woman makes me different. That difference maps the race and gender hierarchies used to justify the marginalization of bodies like mine across the globe for five hundred years. It is inescapable, so instead of trying to outrun my body, I spent the first twenty-five years of life studying its tendencies intensely, learning to constrain it, and trying to make it—instead of a body exuding a menacing strength—not even a body, just some impossible space-saving vapor.

I tried to starve myself into a new, more acceptable white body type and drove myself crazy during my teens and early twenties questioning why my body didn't meet the standards set by the white community around me, including a six-month period where I subsisted, foolishly, on six hundred calories per day. And I did all of this because at school my body also signaled to the mostly white boys around me that I was off-limits, impossible to introduce to anyone of consequence as a girlfriend, and therefore, almost invisible—at least in the ways teenage girls want. So, I, like so many Black girls attending predominantly white high schools, found a Black boyfriend, Michael, at another predominantly white school. My relationship with my now husband Michael provided respite from the all-white social circles to which I was limited. But it also created the bifurcation of my psyche, then manifested squarely in my perception of my body.

At school, I adorned myself in order to belong. I worked jobs in retail for the discount so I could better perform belonging where I increasingly felt out of place. I was (and still am) a terrible makeup artist, so I depended on my clothes and hair to position myself within white standards of beauty and to illustrate my belonging in predominantly white settings. The six weeks I spent folding clothes at the Gap in 2000 were mind-numbing, but worth the 40 percent employee discount to pay for clothes that would help me fit in, to transform me from a "sacred Black cow" to just another student. By contrast, in predominantly Black spaces I was aware of my body in a different way, aware of my increased sense of comfort and reduced levels of anxiety as my whole body slowly unclenched. These Black people, part of my cultural community, don't care about the white-washed adornment of the Gap, and they took offense to the idea that I, or any of us, should fade into the white world around us. With them I laugh fully and talk loudly, and together we reflect our true selves, and show off our strength.

But Black communities, too, police the bodies of Black women. My maternal family members are all naturally short, small-boned women, and I've spent a lifetime coming to terms with the space I take up in comparison to them. In fact, I spent a lot of my teenage years reacting to the astonishment with which people regarded me in relation to them, especially my small, beautiful mother. My mom's small frame and striking beauty attracted attention that positioned me as the anti-beauty to her Black '90s "it-girl." Her long hair, colored contacts, and petite stature positioned her in closer relationship to white standards of beauty than any other Black woman I knew. My inability to match her body's size and acceptability felt suffocating to me, a little Black girl desperate for validation of my body's membership within the mostly white social settings I tried to enter.

At the same time, as my mother's daughter, I did inherit her "brown beauty" and the perceptions of Black middle-class stability, respectability, and attractiveness mapped onto "brownness" during the Harlem Renaissance.[5] Being "brown" has positively impacted my experiences in public settings, especially predominantly white ones. On the spectrum of skin tone, my brown skin is more socially acceptable than darker shades of brown and black—a shade Du Bois used to point to, as editor of *The Crisis* magazine, as the best and most noncontroversial representations of Black excellence. I am undeniably Black, but not so dark that I'm reduced to color only. Skin tone matters, and as mine projected my Blackness to my peers, it also positioned me as socially acceptable and sexually available in ways I didn't realize.

Abuses

In high school, my relationships with white men transformed from asexual, where my presence as a potential love interest was basically ignored, to relationships based almost solely on sexually suggestive touching, comments, and, in one odd case, the gifting of black lace lingerie that (eerily) fit perfectly.

"What is this?" I asked, simultaneously tearing the wrapping paper off my gift to reveal a series of square plastic bags. I wasn't expecting any gifts from the white man sitting next to me, but also never turned down a present, so I was eager—and a little frightened—to see what he'd gotten me. "Just a Christmas present," he replied with a tone implying something more sinister. I examined the bags closely before opening them, their contents obscured by the night's darkness and low dashboard light of the car in which we were sitting. I had driven myself, but he'd lured me into his car with promises of gifts. I picked the biggest bag, and as I freed the fabric from its plastic casing, I realized it was a Black lace push-up bra from *Victoria's Secret*. My heart sank. This was completely inappropriate and unexpected from this man, someone with whom I'd been friends and only friends for almost six years.

I suppose I shouldn't have been surprised; he was notoriously touchy with women, but he always took it to another level with me, saying and doing things like gifting me this bra—along with the matching panties and garter belt inside the other bags—daring me to accuse him of nefarious intentions. He wouldn't dare do anything like this to our shared white girl friends, as evidenced by the horrified looks on their faces as I relayed the story to each and every one of them. But their horror didn't mean these white women, my friends, understood the terrorism of having to deal with constant and intense hyper-sexualization, nor did I have the right words to explain it to them. "Just don't talk to him anymore," they suggested as though he were a lone crazed wolf, rather than yet another example of white men's assumption of access to my body based on one hundred years of white supremacist sexual violation of Black women. He wouldn't be the first or last white man to treat me this way.

The lack of a formal campus police force at Vassar decreased my potential for exposure to capital violence while attending college, but it also increased my exposure to sexual violence. The combination of drugs, alcohol, and minimal supervision creates environments where the powerful can prey on the powerless. White men retain power via money and status on campus that, at many schools, allows them to prey on women unencumbered. This isn't theory. Fraternities at Temple University,[6] Indiana University,[7] University of Michigan,[8] and Dartmouth College[9] were removed from campus after multiple accusations of sexual assault and rape by members and at official fraternity events. Twenty-three percent of women on college campuses experience rape or sexual assault, compared to 5 percent of men.[10]

Seventy-eight percent of reports of rape and assault on college campuses are made by white women, but Black women are more likely to be abused in these settings. I was one of the Black women whose abuse went unreported. But it didn't go undiscussed. I told my friends, mutual friends shared with my abuser, and even my student fellow (Vassar's less authoritative version of resident advisor), all of whom advised me not to escalate the situation, to just ignore him, not unlike what my high school girlfriends told me to do about another white male line-stepper. It never occurred to them that I might be suffering. The main focus was maintaining relationships going forward, my own trauma be damned.

The hyper-sexualization I experienced in college didn't begin with my sexual assault, but it escalated from public interactions to incidents of harassment quickly. Being sexually assaulted wouldn't even be the apex of the sexual trauma I'd experience on campus grounds, but it was the thing that made me realize I was marked as usable for sexual experimentation without my permission in that space, the Black women on which men—and sometimes women—could freely map previously unexplored desires, with my permission or without it. The trauma of this knowledge is not just in the understanding of my position but in the seclusion required to stay safe.

Whenever the memory hits me again, as I'm driving in my car, teaching a class, or reading a book, I remember the fear I felt as his hands disturbed my sleep, the lump in my throat that appeared out of nowhere and forced me to choke back the tears in my eyes and the cries in my chest. It wasn't the first time I'd felt violated, I'd been subjected to more benign sexual harassment on the street or at parties, but this was my first exposure to sexual abuse, and the first time I felt powerless to change my immediate circumstances.

I never cried. I never yelled. I never said *stop*. I just lay there, pretending to be asleep, willing him to stop until I mustered up the courage to do the only thing I could think of in that moment. I rolled over, forcing him to stop by cutting off the angle his arms were using to reach me. I waited a few more beats, maybe ninety seconds, before I got up and went back down the hall to my room, where my roommate was in bed watching the movie I'd passed up to hang with our friend.

On historically white-serving campuses, the fetishization of Black and brown women is common and leads to our higher rates of assault. Less than eighteen months after my sexual assault, on the eve of my twentieth birthday, I woke up to find another white man in my dorm room, uninvited in the middle of the night. I struggled to release myself from the grip he had me in, begging him to let me go as he tried harder to land the kiss I was struggling against. In the end, it was my tears, falling onto my cheeks as I questioned why he was doing this to me, his supposed friend, that made him stop and eventually leave me, traumatized but physically unharmed. I locked my door every night after that.

Sexual expectations are mapped onto Black women's bodies without our consent. Our identities, but not our bodies, are relegated to the background in most public spaces, so colonizers' can over-sexualize, objectify, and "other" our bodies without ever taking us seriously as individuals. It was at HWSCUs that I learned the possible traumas of hyper-visibility for Black women and the physical and physiological destruction of the self that happens to us there. The condemnation of Black women in American society simultaneously makes us targets for sexual conquests among young white men, perpetuating the legacies of their colonizing forefathers, and social lepers ostracized from committed monogamous relationships with the same men.

There are few words for the confusion and pain that come from realizing most of the white, cis, het men you call friends are more interested in the prospect of a sexual experience with a Black woman than making a legitimate friend connection. A check on the college bucket list tucked neatly in the back pocket of their jeans the day they arrived on campus, Black women are objects for discovery, not people to be known. To experience sexual control over a Black woman's body is a goal often discussed freely among white men eager to experience the rush of engaging in the social taboo of interracial hookups. I was available for sex if I was open to it, and sexual abuse if I was not; in this I had little choice.

None of the white men I encountered on campus were actually interested in getting to know me beyond the relationship between what they had heard about Black women and what they experienced with one in the flesh. They wanted to explore us, our bodies in particular. The white men I encountered in college wanted to devour every inch of what made me a Black woman. To them, Black women were mystical creatures yet to be explored, a potential tangle of taboos and temptations held out of reach for them in childhood, suddenly available and coercible.

Pain

Young Black girls are more likely to self-harm than white girls, but they're much less likely to receive treatment.[11] This is not a coincidence. Pain moves through the body strategically, warning us of danger and suggesting caution, a perfect coping mechanism. I used pain to shock myself out of the unremitting anxiety and nagging depression that showed up after my sexual assault. Sometimes those old friends—anxiety and depression—still make me feel as though I'm drowning where I stand. Handling the constant social surveillance of this body, the feeling of eyes on me as I have tried to live in peace, was a difficult weight for me to carry, and for a time I only found solace in inflicting visceral, tangible pain on myself by cutting. Part punishment, part distraction from other traumas, this self-destructive behavior seemed a reasonable response at the time. I ended up in therapy six months after it started when a professor noticed the growing number of scars on my forearms. It is work I continue regularly to this day.

The adrenaline rush of seeing my warm, dark blood seep from the razor-thin cuts on my arm, the sting of the open wound exposed to the elements, and the immediate clarity of mind to know how to care for my wound provided small moments of peace. In those moments, the world regained its order. I had the knowledge and the power to improve my circumstances. The pain provided a path through the darkness into the light. Black women derive strength from our bodies, but we're also persecuted by them.

I don't glorify cutting, but I understand it now as a physical manifestation of unresolved oppression. I didn't understand then how my race and the race of the white men I interacted with in college dictated the particulars of my subjugation. I just felt unbalanced, constantly off-center, as if the force of being hyper-sexualized literally knocked me off my spot. The pain helped me focus on tethering my physical body to the ground underneath me when it might be easier to float away.

Still naive to the complexities of racialization and the stigma of being a Black woman in America, I came to college unprepared for the fetishizing of my body. Entering a space of overt fetishizing turned my world upside down. I'd later come to understand that *this* was right side up, I'd just not seen it before. I looked to my body to offer some control in an environment where everything felt completely out of control. Robbed of self-esteem and stunted by a crumbling self-concept, it's easy to feel alone. My body provided relief and comfort when it felt so elusive. And in the physical pain I inflicted on myself I found a destructive solace.

The fault was mine. I took the white men around me at their word, the same mistake made by the ancestors of so many communities of color. I ignored my previous experiences and assumed them sincere, for which I paid my fair share in heartache. Back then, I was first shocked, then intrigued by the constant attention from the white men around me. Because I thought them genuine, every ounce of attention seemed to position me a little closer to traditional white standards of beauty, to finally make me the Vassar girl I longed to be.

By the time I realized the farce, that these men were not, in fact, genuine, I had already made myself vulnerable, called them my friends. Every cut on my arm in the subsequent years was self-inflicted punishment for trusting those who could never have my best interest at heart, a reminder of the callous ways my body was treated, the unwanted touching and inappropriate comments.

The blatant disregard for the boundaries I set as a woman—a Black woman—made every space I entered a potentially dangerous one. As if I were an off-duty cab driving through Manhattan in the rain, white men were constantly trying to flag me down regardless of the lack of interest or availability I asserted. I could not say enough or withdraw enough to ensure my peace or my safety. I found myself not only subject to the constant and aggressive white male gaze but subject to their whims as well. Saartjie Baartman tried to find some power in the objectification of her body but depended on heavy alcohol use to numb life in the spotlight as a "freak." She died at twenty-six years of age from complications of illness and alcoholism—her chosen method of coping and her eventual destruction. We all find our own, often destructive ways to cope with the life of hyper-visibility.

In the community of small, dark scar tissue giving away the identity of my accomplice, a razor blade I kept in my sock drawer and took out whenever I felt too much, shows the physical damage of living in this body. They are tangible manifestations of moving through the world in a body simultaneously maligned and obsessed over. Now faded, their disappearance over time does not lessen the pain of the foundations that led to them. My scars are visceral reminders of how easy it is for a Black woman to be engulfed by such unnatural obsessions with our bodies and the pain of the required dualism to be hyper-visible, and inherently unacceptable.

Marked

The intensity of the white male gaze marks Black women as things to be consumed and discarded. Even as white people observe and appropriate all those pieces of the Black female body deemed too different from white bodies, Black women reap no benefits. We cannot escape the scrutiny of our lips or our hips while white mimicry of the same features is glorified. The loneliness accompanying existence in a world where the only social value you derive is infused in your physical body and its usefulness to uplifting whiteness leaves many Black women with deep, profound emotional and psychological scarring. In predominantly white spaces where surveillance is unavoidable, my awareness of Black women's physical subjugation awoke, and simultaneously my trust in the folks around me eroded.

I remember distinctly, at twenty years old, feeling lonely and depressed as awareness of my body's hyper-visibility isolated me from the people and places where I derived joy. My brain was in overdrive with paranoia, imagining infinite angles at which the men around me were considering my body, and I grew highly anxious in public settings, especially on campus. In the preceding years, I had learned very little about my worth outside of my intellect, only to be met in college with objectification that called into question my belonging in this setting, academics be damned. It was impossible to explain to my white girlfriends then, just as it is now, exactly why and how I feel this way, which caused an additional need to withdraw. Many days it seemed easier to stay in bed than to deal with the reality of walking across campus in this body, forever in the spotlight. I felt alone and out of place in the only setting where I wanted to truly belong, trapped in a body I only ever felt like escaping.

I should have looked to my mother for support and explained to her what was happening to me and what had already happened to me. I should've asked her how to grieve the soul and intellect that used to move me before all this, before I came to know myself as just a form—usable but unnecessary. I'd never considered that my mother struggled through the world in this marked body just as I did. As a Black woman attending a Wisconsin college in the mid-1970s, the socially constructed burden of her body, however more petite and desirable in nature, was no less violent in its wrath. But we haven't yet figured out how to collectively communicate our shared pain, so instead Black women (especially mothers and daughters) often suffer silently, side by side, choking on our embarrassment in trusting whiteness as we continue to endure its supremacy, as my mother and I did for a time.

The mutual understanding of the damning nature of our bodies is at the heart of the constant clash of egos mirrored in so many relationships between Black mothers and daughters. It's only recently that I even revealed my sexual assault to my mother. I was too ashamed of what it might say to her about me, that I had allowed myself to be put in that situation. But her shock and anger at my revelation almost twenty years later was evidence that she understood me as the victim, well aware of how Black women are victimized by white men in predominantly white settings.

We share a visceral understanding of the weight of being a Black woman in America. Our bodies, heavy with the encumbrance of intersectionality, are dominated and castrated by the very institutions that define us. To every person we meet, Black women are at first, sometimes ever, only bodies. Establishing our bodies as the foundation of Black women's social value in a society where the possible social value of those bodies is meager at best encourages us to misuse and abuse them and to allow abuse where white women do not.

I came to understand myself during my college years as just a body, a mistake it would take me, and my therapists—plural—a long time to repair. Reimagining my body as a husk, a shell that I could detach from, lessened the sting of constant reminders from those around me that my body was the most visible in the room. None of this made me feel particularly attractive. I learned quickly that my body's hyper-visibility had little connection to individual opinions of how cute I was, or was not. I am marked by race. Men, and women, touch me without permission, whether admiring my hair, tattoos, clothes (and oddly, my dog), people find all sorts of completely irrational reasons to subject my body to their whims. The danger in the routine nature of this consistent objectification is how quickly it joins a host of other normative expectations unique to being Black and a woman. When you get used to being treated as a body first, but rarely a complete person, subsequent decision-making is skewed. Or maybe that's just me.

7

Class Matters

I begged for a car for months after I passed my driving test and celebrated my sixteenth birthday, but it was an entire year before my mom came home one afternoon to announce she'd found me transportation, and that we should go look at it together before she signed the title. The 1989 white Honda Civic was everything I wanted: four doors, a clean interior, working heat and air-conditioning, and less than one hundred thousand miles. My retail paychecks from the plethora of after-school jobs I worked weren't nearly enough to cover the $2,500 price tag, but my mother and I agreed that a car would mean I could help run errands and shuffle my little sister around when she was busy with work. So as long as I covered the gas and took care of the car's general upkeep, she would gift me the car. In my excitement at the thought of the freedom I was about to access, I didn't notice until the test drive that the car indeed had a flaw: it was a manual transmission. "Learn to drive it, or keep taking the bus," my mother responded to my pleas to keep looking for an automatic.

So I set about teaching myself, via a combination of Google and *Driving Stick for Dummies*, to drive my newly acquired car. Very few of my driving-age cousins had cars at all, so my new vehicle ownership marked a clear class difference between us. I spent my afternoons teaching myself to drive stick. I marked my speedometer with tape as a reminder of when to shift, and I maneuvered slowly around the parking lot of my condo complex practicing, determined to learn to drive it and fully step in to my identity as teenage car owner.

But at school, my car marked my class in a different way. It was older, didn't always start on the first try, and was outfitted with tropical print seat covers I bought at *Hot Topic* to cover the existing tears in the seat cushions. I replaced the old AM/FM radio with a CD player, but she still looked pitiful next to many of the other students' cars. As my friends zipped around town easily in their much newer automatic transmissions, my car was representative of the tenuousness of middle-class identity for many Black folks. My parents made just enough money to buy their way into increasingly middle-class, predominantly white neighborhoods, but our race meant many of our neighbors just assumed we did not belong, and my old car reaffirmed that belief for them. But among our families, we—my mother especially—were a symbol of success. To them, we were the epitome of Black middle-class Cosby-hood, seeing Broadway shows and taking trips overseas.

The symbolic nature of class identity is as important to class membership as actual income and wealth generation. This is especially true for Black folks who never get the benefit of the doubt in assumptions of class membership. The one inherent truth missing from journalistic and political calls to understand the lives of poor white people in this country is the basic invisibility of white poverty. To be white means to be assumed at least middle-class, a social fact that imbues privilege in nonquantifiable ways. In my middle-class community, it meant white families could actually be members of the lower class and the working poor but still have access to high-quality public schools in the area and feel as though they, and their children, belong.

At my predominantly white high school, my car was just another reminder to my peers that I didn't belong, never mind that some of them drove cars older and more beat up than mine. My Blackness was the first strike, as a skin color already deemed deviant; my hair (which couldn't be washed every day and often changed in presentation) was strike two; and this car, of which I was so proud and still think of fondly (both because of how I got it and the work I put in to learn how to drive it) was the final strike—the triumvirate of non-belonging. I may have been middle-class, but not middle-class enough to overcome the penalties of my race, and less middle-class than the dreams transmuted onto us by our Black families.

Blue-Ribbon Districts

Though my mother, sister, and I moved around a lot as my mother chased promotions to improve our class status, both children, my sister Jenaé and I, spent the majority of our K through 12 years in one district, Independent School District (IDS) 196. The fourth-largest school district in Minnesota, IDS 196 includes the suburbs south of the Mississippi River and is less than twenty miles from the twin cities of Minneapolis and Saint Paul. When I attended in the middle and late 1990s, IDS 196 was considered one of the best school districts in the country, and Apple Valley High School, one of the best 140 high schools in the United States.[1] The district has been awarded six National Blue Ribbon awards for excellence, given to the highest performing schools based on state assessments in academics, athletics, and the arts. More importantly, thanks to Minnesota's system of relying on local property taxes to fund school districts (which is not unlike many other states) and the high property values of the upper middle class homes in the area, IDS 196 has historically had a surplus of budgetary funds to allocate per student.

My mom understood the game. Find a public school in a well-funded district, and rent within district lines. Though my mom always coveted ownership (and she did eventually buy a house in the district in 2003), renting was a way in, when she'd otherwise be unable to afford to send us to schools of this caliber. Her strategy was well founded. Renting meant flexibility when we inevitably moved states so she could move up the corporate ladder, but it also made access to well-funded public schools a reality for her children. The sad fact about American public education is that continuing to rely on property taxes, and therefore home value, as a major component of public education funding means most Black people won't have access to the best public schools because not only are we less likely to own homes,[2] but when we do those homes are likely worth less and in closer proximity to poor neighborhoods than white people.[3] Stories of Black women using false addresses to enroll their kids in specific schools are more an example of a broken system than an indictment of the mothers in search of quality education for their children. The real crime is that so many Black mothers are forced to resort to these kinds of strategies in the first place when white mothers are not.

The perpetual imbalance of per-student funding district-to-district is not indicative of a flaw in the system. The system was built this way on purpose. The first iteration of what would become our modern public education institution proposed by Thomas Jefferson included a two-track system to separate students into "the laboring and learned," where the majority find themselves in the former and a select few "geniuses" would be afforded upward social mobility as the "learned" via more formal education.[4] A few years later, situating education around residential land occupation and therefore positioning non-white settlers as unworthy of education, the "survey" of the Northwest Territory (what would later become a handful of midwestern states, including Dakota County, Minnesota, named for the tribe of Native Americans displaced by white occupation) established townships across the land and reserved space for local schools in each area via land grants. This occupation of land already in use by Native Americans was also the impetus for establishing white supremacy as a part of the fabric of American development and inherent to a lack of belonging among non-white students for the next three centuries.

Dividing American land into towns was foundational to shaping the United States into classed communities. These "towns" maintain inequality in public education that specifically disadvantages poor Black and brown students while providing state-funded advantages to rich white students. By 1830, Massachusetts passed laws to provide free public education to all children, including the first public high school, and fourteen years later the state would legalize segregated schools ahead of Black emancipation,[5] though more than 5 percent of enslaved people would still learn to read at the risk of severe physical punishment or death.[6]

During the industrial revolution, public schools were meant to create docile, obedient factory workers out of the white and increasingly immigrant populations swelling American cities. The necessity to "civilize" immigrants led to the passing of compulsory education laws designed to make them better workers and simultaneously force the learning and use of English as the primary language in public settings. These requirements formalize non-white students as the other, whose belonging is proven via successful assimilation into public spaces designed around the needs of white men. It forces non-white students to mirror their white peers rather than advocate for their unique interests.

In 1837, Horace Mann became the first head of the Massachusetts State Board of Education,[7] a state enterprise under which Mann championed public education for all.* Ironically, Horace Mann's namesake, the Horace Mann School in New York City, is the second most expensive private school in the area and caters to the richest and wealthiest predominantly white students. The tuition for 2018–2019 was $51,000 per K through 12 academic year. In 2010, Horace Mann School was named the second-best prep school in the country by *Forbes* magazine,[8] hardly the free common public education first imagined by Mann, and evidence of the class-based nature of American education.

Today public education is segregated as much by class as it is by race, with the wealthiest families—the majority white—accessing the highest quality education. In the years between Mann's development of public education in Massachusetts and the introduction of public education's modern template, an equation of funding was developed out of varying mixes of federal, state, and local sources. In 2022, federal funding equaled about 10 percent of a school district's overall budget, regardless of the state. The rest of the money comes from a percentage of sales and income tax revenue from the state and often, most importantly, from local district communities.

A combination of state and local funding racializes public schooling because neighborhoods and, thus, neighborhood home

---

* Mann also pushed for gender teaching, transforming it into a "feminine" profession because he felt women were better suited for teaching.

values are in part decided by the racial makeup of the area. Redlining was the primary tool local governments used to create "white" and "Black" neighborhoods and install "good" and "bad" schools within their borders.[9] Fifty years of constricted mortgage approvals in predominantly Black neighborhoods led to white flight from integrating neighborhoods as Black people took on predatory loans to access home ownership in which the values of their homes would never appreciate. Today, modern gentrification continues to displace Black folks in areas where home prices are low but because of government subsidies on local property taxes. This doesn't improve the funding scenarios in the same neighborhoods, leaving Black people living in predominantly Black communities gutted by poverty and therefore without access to quality public education compared to their white peers in well-funded neighborhoods. Even with incomes of more than $75,000, Black households are more likely located in higher poverty neighborhoods than white households earning less than $40,000. We are being purposefully herded into impoverished communities and blocked from the many institutions that may precipitate our escape.

I recognize that I benefited from a system of public education specifically meant *not* to benefit Black families or the children they need to educate. But the totality of public educational structure and the culture it perpetuates meant that while I can and do access higher quality education than a majority of Black people in this country, it's not enough to make me belong there. And perceived belonging, as we have seen, is important to several facets of academic achievement. Imagine understanding that the classrooms you occupy are not spaces built with your needs or education in mind, and simultaneously understanding the amount of "Black excellence" necessary to justify your presence to your white teachers, counselors, and administrators—justifications not expected of your white classmates, regardless of their class identity. Sometimes, parents (like mine) try to make the best decisions to ensure the most positive outcomes for their kids, so they overlook the traumas their children will be exposed to in the interest of better long-term life chances. I was successful, but not everyone is. What looks like upward social mobility for the Black middle class in the eyes of Black people without the same class access is actually static positioning, and includes perpetual feelings of unwelcomeness in the institutions and entrance into predominantly white classrooms we need simply to maintain our livelihoods. Once inside HWSCUs, excessive academic achievements lead to only minimal potential upward social mobility, and downward mobility is just a few missed paychecks away.

The Vassar Curve

The fact that I wanted so badly to take my beloved car to college with me speaks to my unfamiliarity with stereotypes of Vassar students before I arrived on campus and my naivete about the salience of symbolic class membership in that setting. The expensive European cars that lined the campus lots were not those of the faculty but the students, and for the first time, I felt ashamed about my own. I was shocked at the feelings of shame that welled inside of me, but this was the start of a lot of confusion about where I belonged and what my class identity really was. It probably had something to do with the class demographics of the campus community. Less than 10 percent of Vassar students were federal Pell Grant recipients (awarded to the students in the bottom 40 percent of income distribution) when I attended.[10] To say Vassar is a wealthy college is an understatement.

College was the first place where I truly felt poor as opposed to having that assumption mapped onto me. I was, despite how other

Black people saw me, just "another Negro from Niggerland." These feelings did not emerge because I identified as such but because the culture of Vassar—not just the people attending—marked me as a member of a substandard class. The class hierarchy of students at HWSCUs isn't always blatant but is embedded into perceptions of belonging. If you're there and you're white, belonging is assumed as part of the expectations of high-class status regardless of your actual class identity. Black and brown students, on the other hand, are immediately outsiders—again, regardless of class—and therefore have to carefully manage our performances to maintain belonging, this also includes a performance of class.

The hardest part about writing this book, really the hardest part of being a Black woman moving through the privileged academic spaces I have, is recognizing the ways in which my class identity (at least a perception of it) has impacted my experiences. This is complicated for many reasons, but the three most important are: (1) My access to "upper-class spaces" is less reflective of my parents' income and more reflective of access to high capital networks, (2) Access to high-capital networks without access to associated amounts of money intensifies feelings of non-belonging, and 3) Regardless of actual class identity, Black people are rarely assumed as upper-class, so performance is required.

I attended Vassar on a 50 percent academic scholarship. Work-study—where I lucked out with a job in the Dean of Studies Office—my parents' financial support, and small federal loans and Pell Grants covered the rest of the tuition and room and board. In 2001–2002—my first year enrolled, the total cost to attend Vassar College was $33,450, and older students were already lamenting the perpetual increase in the cost to attend. In fact, while I was worried about high school graduation the spring before, already enrolled students were angry about the 5 percent cost increase coming the following year.[11] Yet even as salaries nationwide have remained flat for almost twenty years since, college attendance rates have skyrocketed along with the cost of attendance.[12] For the 2022–2023 academic year Vassar's attendance cost $81,360—$48,000 more per year than I spent twenty-one years earlier.

The cost of higher education creates a tenuous relationship between race, education, and class identity because assumptions of income associated with jobs that require advanced education are no longer based on reality, especially for Black workers. Attending Vassar for undergrad only left me $20,000 in debt—still a devastating amount of money for a Black woman to owe given that I'm already likely to earn less than white and Asian people of any gender, and even my Black men counterparts. That devastation was compounded by the fact that the average salary for liberal arts graduates in 2005 was $30,337.[13]

More than many of my white peers, I *needed* to go to Vassar. I understood that a bachelor's degree from an unknown college or state university wasn't going to make me marketable enough to maintain my middle-class membership. It wasn't my first choice, but the more I learned about the college, the more I realized that I needed the alumni networks, faculty connections, and brand name to overcome the obstacles of my race and class identities. Sure, lots of students *wanted* those things, and I suspected—not unlike the students of the 2019 Operation Varsity Blues scandal—that at least some of my white peers were admitted for reasons other than objective admissions requirements, enough to create a clear class identity within the campus community. But many of them, like my fellow Vassar undergrads, didn't actually need to attend a prestigious school to maintain the lifestyles in which they'd grown up. So I went into debt early in life, essentially buying my way in all the same—except that *I* couldn't really afford it.

Today, first-generation academics are quickly vanishing from higher education.[14] Even if one wanted to use education as a tool for upward social mobility, they're likely simultaneously trapping themselves into a lifetime of debt, with no real increase in wages to pay it off. President Biden's 2022 student loan forgiveness changes the lives of so many college-educated Black folks trapped in perpetual student loan debt. It doesn't change my personal circumstances because I also went on to get a doctorate, and even on fellowship that degree was three times the cost of my undergraduate degree. How many of us Black faculty went into heavy debt to earn doctoral degrees? The answer is a lot.

That's a hard thing to admit while also trying to fit in among a class of people who rarely think about money as a limited resource, and never think about race as a hindrance to their belonging—anywhere. And I was often seduced by the desire to hang with my friends, to belong in this space and with these people with whom I shouldn't belong. It cost me. By the time I graduated, I was already several thousand dollars in credit card debt, having been the perfect prey for those companies who elected to camp out in university commons offering "free" money to those who needed it, and don't really understand the consequences of their early financial decisions.

Class identity was subtle though. Students didn't walk around with their net worth pinned to their cashmere sweaters. Instead, the assumption of at least an upper middle class identity was underlying every conversation, every extracurricular activity. (I won't say how much debt I went in to traveling to Australia with the rugby team one spring break.) To out yourself as a usurper meant to permanently impact social interactions and subsequent benefits going forward. In short, you'd stop getting invited to "stuff." From a cost-analysis perspective, it made more sense to try to fit in.

Who Are You?

Early in my freshman year, a Black security guard stopped me as I drunkenly cut through a closed dining hall in an effort to reach my dorm room, the location of which was still a bit foreign to me. "Hey," he beckoned as I moved wobbly, head down through the (maybe) closed room. I took a few more steps trying to discern if it was me he was talking to, before I stopped, turned, and look toward the unknown voice. He introduced himself before saying something along the lines of, "That *Unbreakable* was so good. Your pops is good, you know." We exchanged a long unbroken stare for a few moments as I tried to process what he said amid the red Solo cups of beer swirling in my head. "I . . . I don't know what you mean. Thanks," I mumbled as I hurried quickly through the nearest exit. As I continued the slow trek to my room, I tried to sift through the previous interaction to figure out what happened, but I came up with nothing before I passed out in my bed and didn't think of it again for several months. The "interaction" and more salient understandings of race, class, and belonging on campus became clear to me when I finally met Zoe. She was the daughter of Samuel L. Jackson, and the only other brown-skinned Black girl on campus wearing micro-braids. Meeting her was something of an epiphany. We don't look alike, but it never occurred to the security guard that I could be a Black woman student on campus whose father *wasn't* worth nine figures, and that mindset was indicative of the importance of class here. If I was going to be Black, I had to at least be upper class.

My experiences are not unique to Black students, especially those of us at private, predominantly white institutions. But as the cost of education at the most prestigious institutions continues to skyrocket, Black students, more than their white peers, use loan funds with long payoff times to cover attendance that now far exceeds the salaries for jobs requiring only bachelor's degrees.[15] The inheritable wealth my friends nonchalantly accessed for mortgage down payments, high credit card limits, and to finance the interim years between graduating college and actually settling on a career helped them build lifestyles to which I didn't have access. Instead, I took out more student loans in an effort to become more marketable on the job market, and then again to get a doctorate and potentially even increase my class status.

In 2016, Black adults still owed a median of 113 percent of their original student loan balance per capita twelve years after starting college. This is compared to white adults who still owed a median of 65 percent of the original balance, leaving more money to build a financially stable life in an economy where wages are flat. This disproportion in student loan debt held, plus the more than $10,000 inheritance that 41 percent of white college-educated families receive on average compared to 13 percent of Black college-educated families means white folks don't have to perform class-based belonging in college, or as they navigate careers that presume high salaries (regardless of the salary itself).[16] This is why total student loan cancellation is an anti-racist issue. It would address some—but not all—of this country's class disparities, rather than simply acting as a tax break for the rich as many conservatives falsely claim. Rich people don't have student loan debt, but families with low wealth do—especially Black families.

At Vassar, class identity is a performance that spans the life of active alumni participation. To continue taking advantage of the capital provided by my attendance, I must maintain a tangible connection to the college, again in ways my fellow white alumni do not. It's not enough to walk around in Vassar-branded clothing, or the women's rugby bag I take to the gym. In fact, when white people ask me about how I procured the aforementioned college "swag," the question that inevitably comes is not *when* I attended Vassar, but who *I know* that did. Attendance is not enough to secure the class identity and accompanying social position the white students get with little additional effort. Instead, Black alumni, especially of prestigious institutions, must constantly reify the relationship between themselves and their respective schools in order to pull even basic forms of capital (a belief that you attended, for example) from the financial investment of higher education. I essentially paid for the right to spend my life and career convincing people that I went to Vassar College, then convincing people I'm a college professor. The predictability of these interactions is always aggravating, and often maddening, as it becomes clear there is nothing I can do, no performance I can put on that would map assumptions of prestigious education onto me, a Black woman.

And it's worth it, even if it's not *worth it*. That's why Black people continue to attend college at higher rates each year, and why rich white people are committing fraud to guarantee their children are admitted to the country's most illustrious institutions. The financial bubble that threatens to take out the knees of our economy via massive student loan defaults in the next decade reflects the utility of college degrees even when it's difficult to assess exactly how much more skilled students are at graduation in comparison to when they arrive—especially in comparison to the cost of attendance.

But successfully completing degrees from these schools starts a chain of events that *can* improve your status and class identity, even if it does not always. In fact, over the last decade, Vassar has committed to decreasing class inequality on campus by offering admitted students 100 percent of needed financial aid. Former Vassar College President Catherine "Cappy" Bond Hill recognized the increasing importance of education as a tool for upward social mobility *and* referenced the overwhelming whiteness of her own alma mater, Williams College, as part of the impetus for doubling the college's financial aid budget in an effort to economically and racially diversify the student population.[17]

The college boasts about the 13 percent increase in students of color in the years following the budget increases beginning in 2012, but the population of Black students has actually decreased as a part of this effort. This happens in part because flat salaries and rising costs of living across the country mean that many people, regardless of race, are more "in need" of financial assistance to attend the most expensive—and often most prestigious—colleges and universities than in the past. But this increase in need across the board doesn't change the inferior wealth position of Black people relative to non-Black people as a result of centuries of disproportionate wages, stunted home ownership, and prohibited education. To focus on erasing class disparities rather than race explicitly advantages non-Black students in the admissions process even more than usual, and makes Black students' presence on campus even less expected or likely.

Black people, more concerned with upward social mobility than increased social status, don't come to attend college as a tacit way to reinforce status, the way the students of Operation Varsity Blues did, or at least their parents did on their behalf. For wealthy non-Black people, prestigious college alumni membership is about the performance of status. For poor and middle-class Black people, on the other hand, it's the potential class identity that is most valuable, and also the most impossible to attain. So, if we happen to make it past the gilded gates and into prestigious—but expensive—schools, of course, we're going to take the financial risk to attend. We can't really afford not to.

Faking It until I Make It

This wallowing in self-pity about my class identity doesn't mean I can't access spaces that should be beyond my means, and it definitely doesn't mean I missed out on opportunities and experiences (see: eleven days in Australia). To even be in a position to perform class belonging above my actual class membership is a measure of privilege. My mother's job did that for us in ways that taught me the intricacies of interactions with people and in spaces where I'm unexpected. In fact, when I was young, I loved to watch her interact with white people and made mental notes when her behavior shifted from who she was in predominantly Black settings to who she was capable of becoming when our belonging was challenged on the basis of racism or sexism—which happened often. My little sister and I could always read the situation and shared stifled laughs in recognition of what was coming next.

As a Black woman born in Arkansas and a part of the second-wave Great Migration, my mother grew up in Milwaukee, Wisconsin, one of the historically ten worst cities for Black people to live in this country and the most segregated city in the United States.[18] Her decision to head west to Madison for college proved to be important to her own potential for upward social mobility, as the city of Milwaukee continued to degrade in the late seventies and eighties, especially North Milwaukee where Black people are concentrated and where she grew up. Any Black woman attending the University of Wisconsin, Madison, in the 1970s would be forced to learn a measure of performance just to be successful there, but it was her decision to become a stewardess (back when they still called them that) that taught her, and by extension my sister and I, the subtle art of performing class belonging in predominantly white spaces. It was my mother's attendance at UW-Madison that shaped both her belief in the necessity of a college degree from a well-ranked school and the reality of life at a historically white-serving institution, especially in the notoriously racist and unwelcoming environment of Madison, Wisconsin.

Tending to the whims of mostly white businessmen for the duration of flights is both terrifying to imagine and perhaps the most efficient way for a Black woman to learn performative belonging in a white upper-class world. It helped that her job came with a status that, if not upper class itself, mimics it quite well. My mother traveled around the world before she was twenty-five years old. My dad and uncles got drunk on liter bottles of sake at my parents' wedding reception that my mom brought back from a work trip to Narita, Japan.

One of only three Black flight attendants in her graduating flight school class (the others were my godmother and their roommate), my mother had to navigate secondhand smoke (on planes, which sounds like a special kind of hell), misogyny, and of course racism from the mostly white businessmen dominating the skies in the seventies and eighties—an unexpected Black woman in what was still a mode of travel focused on the white upper class. But it was a mutually beneficial relationship between her and the airline that was looking to diversify. She spent her twenties and early thirties traveling throughout Europe and Asia, picking up bits of the languages, cultures, and styles along the way. That job, and those that followed, allowed my sister and me opportunities to do the same.

This is where class gets complicated for me. My family's ability to move across class borders in ways many Black people are never allowed doesn't change that we experience racism in those settings. There is privilege in gaining entrance to upper-class spaces, but there's also violence. My mother's career allowed us to travel around the world, and often in first class, but we were still told by white passengers that we were in the wrong line and were asked to show our boarding passes when we took our assigned seats. It paid enough to allow us entrance into the best public school districts, but meant our abilities were constantly undervalued, we were disciplined more harshly and had to aggressively advocate for ourselves to make sure we were competitive with our white peers for college admissions.

Vitriol for the Black middle class is especially intense among the white working poor, who have been raised to measure their upward class progress against the class identity of the Black people around them.[19] Upper-class white people, on the other hand, view us with disdain at best, but usually something between sympathy and apathy, because we're not a threat to their existence; we're an annoyance to be tolerated. Really, being Black middle class taught me that regardless of my class, or the class identity of the white people around me, I would never be allowed full class membership to any class except the lowest ones. More importantly, I learned that despite how well I did in school, how many languages I learned, or how many degrees I earned, perceptions of my class status change even slower than my actual class status. "My race is my class and my class is my race," is a conundrum particular to Black folks.

This convergence of race and class is not viewed the same way within Black communities as it is outside them. The Black "upper class" have long been imagined as saviors, redistributing their wealth and resources to less fortunate Black people starting with Du Bois's belief in the role of the "talented tenth" in providing community-wide uplift through higher education. Du Bois believed in the importance of ensuring higher education for the most talented Black people and subsequently focusing the rest of the population toward vocational education and trade work. His theory was born of the belief that it was Black people's long blockage from higher education that inhibited upward social mobility. Moreover, Du Bois, in his infamous rhetorical disagreements with Booker T. Washington, pushed the connections between educating the talented tenth and the potential for Black community uplift. In my own family, I've been singled out by older relatives committed to reminding me of my responsibility to family now that I've "made it," and even though their perception of making it and my financial, emotional, and professional realities are far apart, the only acceptable answer is OK—regardless of what I can actually afford. My career as a college professor, and the class status associated with it (much like my mother's) blurs the line between assumptions of race-based belonging in particularly "upper-class" settings, and the performance of class identity for middle-class Black folks.

Less than 3 percent of Black people earn $200,000 a year or more, an income that can drastically change class identity, depending on the city. Likewise, the median net worth of the top 1 percent of Black wealth-holders is just $1.2 million, and Black college degree holders' median net worth is just $36,800.[20] My net worth is approximately -$221,000,* and I have the highest degree of any living member of my family. I'm also one of the most financially unstable, but the class status associated with my career misrepresents reality. With my family, then, I'm left either divulging my shameful credit report whenever money comes up, or remaining silent and letting assumptions of my class identity distort my economic power.

That doesn't mean I'll be poor forever, though my $200,000 in student loan debt means I may never establish any real inheritable wealth for my future children. If I hustle hard enough to get tenure, publish a few books, maybe—if I'm lucky—I'll direct a center or score an endowed chair later in my career, but regardless of race, being an academic is a test of perseverance, paperwork, and social

---

* Perhaps my debt will be $10,000 less after President Biden's student loan forgiveness policy is applied to my accounts.

networks. The expectation of Black grit, where Black people are doomed to a life of struggle and attempts to overcome perpetual disadvantages—coupled with the academic culture of grit—is also taking years off my life, I'm sure. How's that for class status?

Moving On Up

In this economy where service jobs requiring a minimum college degree are flooding the labor market—in many cases permanently replacing manufacturing jobs requiring only high school education—the $40,000 increase in higher education costs at Vassar indicates increasing difficulty for Black people to use education as a tool for upward class mobility. Already saddled with an insurmountable amount of "bad debt" accumulated just to cover basic life needs like food, clothing, and shelter, and without the support of intergenerational inheritance or economic support available via family and friends, a 118 percent increase in tuition doesn't automatically remove the necessity of a college degree from Black livelihoods.

The largest increases in college tuition happened in the years during and following the Great Recession, when private, nonprofit four-year institutions raised tuition and fees by 5.9 percent. Public four-year colleges saw a 9.5 percent increase, and public two-year colleges saw a whopping 10.2 percent hike.[21] Those increases disproportionately penalized Black students who are entering college in rising numbers but are more likely to come from families unable to support the growing cost of higher education. Black families likely already have extractive debt that doesn't improve credit scores or Black livelihoods, like high-risk mortgages, high-interest credit card debt, and—increasingly likely—student loan debt of their own.[22] White families also have debt, but their debt is likely to increase wealth via low-interest mortgages, credit lines, and home improvement loans. On paper, there is little difference between Black and white families' ability to "afford" college when comparing the amount of debt; in fact, Black families have about half the total debt of white families. But because white debt is so often "good debt," it actually works to improve their lives and the likelihood of access to additional resources, and does not negatively affect long-term economic stability.

This difference in economic position means white students can absorb the financial impact of taking on student loan debt in ways Black students cannot. Huge increases in college tuition prices in an economy that almost demands college degrees for most white-collar, full-time jobs don't decrease the value of the degree in the minds of Black applicants starting from a position of economic disadvantage and looking for a literal change in fortunes. There are also fewer opportunities to drop out and chase entrepreneurship with support from family—financial and emotional—for Black students, even as white millennials and Gen-Zers increasingly chase this life path and find success. So Black people, with fewer available paths to improving class status, rely more heavily on college degrees to jumpstart that process, taking on additional "bad debt" and stunting their present and future economic positions at the same time.

I was fortunate that my parents were able to supplement my undergraduate scholarships with a small amount of their own money to fund my college education, but the reality is that even if they had been unable to provide any financial support, I'd still have attended Vassar and taken the hit to my finances. Without that degree, the likelihood that I would even be in the position I am—not having amassed wealth, but having achieved financial stability, would be slim to none. I'd love to purchase a home, be able to afford extracurricular activities for my children (afford children at all, really), to have enough savings that most emergencies won't immediately plummet my family into financial disrepair. It's a small dream, but something most Black people will never experience.

Our faith in college degrees to save us as individuals and Black communities collectively is a modern manifestation of Du Bois's "Talented Tenth." The remnants of this belief, that Black people need higher education to improve status in society, is made real by twenty-first-century capitalism, but instead of tuition increases pricing Black students out of college, it's simply ensuring the unlikeliness that the degree will actually improve our financial lives.

The most depressing part of all of this is that there is little opportunity to effect change, even if and when a select few of us are able to translate education into economic prosperity. The Great Recession, while also being a time of the greatest tuition increases, was also the catalyst for the gutting of the Black middle class we're so intent on joining. Black families' median net worth was cut in half from $12,000 pre-Great Recession to less than $6,000 post-Great Recession. White families' median net worth, on the other hand, dropped only 11 percent and remained strong at $113,000.[23] Likewise, Black homeownership dropped almost 13 percent post-Great Recession compared to a 2 percent drop in white homeownership, and a 4 percent drop in Latinx ownership over the same time period.[24] Black people are increasingly unable to amass the savings necessary to purchase a home, even less so in a district with high-quality public schools. So, Black students use higher education and the promised potential for upward social mobility to bridge the gap that began with the inequality of K through 12 education.

Class identity, college attendance, and debt, then, are entangled in a vicious cycle of disadvantage and non-belonging for Black folks in the United States. If we get college degrees, we're dooming ourselves to a life of "bad debt," incongruent with public assumptions about our class identity specifically on the basis of education. If we don't go to college, our income and wealth potential plummets, essentially eliminating the possibility of a comfortable economic life barring life-changing luck. Entering the ivory tower, however, means subjection to racism and discrimination that requires a well-rehearsed, class-based performance of belonging and takes a physical and emotional toll. I didn't go to college to go into debt, and my debt is never assumed as a function of my educational achievements. But I am in debt nevertheless and I have to come to terms with the fact that my financial reality may never live up to the collective expectations of a Vassar girl.

8

Benediction

"So, you're quitting the job where you just got a promotion and leaving the city you love to go back to school?" my dad questioned over the phone as I hiked up the hill toward my San Francisco apartment. I'd called on the walk home from work because I knew this would be a frustrating conversation, and I didn't want to do it at work where there were no walls or at home with my unpredictable roommate. The conversation, however, was going worse than expected, so I took a deep breath and again tried to explain my decision to pursue a PhD and what I could potentially achieve as a result. My dad though, who never attended college, was focused on the money I was leaving on the table, the career I'd already begun, and—perhaps most importantly to him—the two degrees I'd already completed (and paid for).

His questions were not unusual, especially for Black PhD candidates. Explaining the necessity of a PhD to communities of people diverted away from higher education for more than a century is difficult. And though the Great Recession wasn't yet in full swing on this day in 2007, it was not lost on my father that a full-time job and thriving career in this economy was a gift to be appreciated rather than cast aside on a whim. Likewise, it's hard to rationalize, especially to a parent, why I would leave a stable situation for a clearly unstable one, to describe my faith in this path in a way that makes sense. Black people are routinely terrorized on predominantly white college campuses, and I experienced my fair share completing my first two degrees, so why keep returning to ground zero? The only answer I ever have is hard for many to comprehend: because I must. This isn't because I feel spiritually "called" to this profession, or think myself uniquely suited to it in any way, but because my obsession with learning and creating knowledge has never waned, regardless of my experiences at school.

I'm not a particularly religious person. I spent a lot of time growing up in the church before I was allowed to make informed decisions about my faith, but since then I've been more jaded than not regarding the usefulness of organized religion compared to an individual's spirituality. And yet, as I wrote this book, I came back time and time again to the concept of benediction to conclude the discussions hopefully sparked by my experiences, and the words I've pieced together to try to describe them. Perhaps that's because of all the things about the church I disliked, the congregation's joint recitation of The Lord's Prayer at the culmination of each Sunday's service was always the headiest part for me. Every member, children and adults, held hands across the sanctuary, and together, in eerily perfect harmony, asked for protection as we left the safety of the surrogate church family and headed back into a dangerous world.

A mix of sweet naivete and resolute faith, I'm not sure I actually felt protected by the prayer itself, even as the words are deeply ingrained in my psyche and easily recalled after fifteen years growing up in "the church." But in church, as in school, we're not completely honest about why we're present, what our presence signals, or the demons we face as a result. The final prayer, then, affirms our faith in some divine protection from those meant to harm us, as well as our own corruptible ambitions. This book exhibits something simultaneously invaluable and incomprehensible about life as a Black woman where we're least expected, the choices we make to survive and excel in predominantly white classrooms. It is a collective prayer for those of us looking for safety and respite from the white supremacist violence of academia, as well as forgiveness for doing what was necessary to maintain access there.

Being Black and a woman in higher education requires faith where it's hard to find. Perhaps in telling our stories, we can continuously manifest that faith for our children who are just now beginning the yearslong journey of institutional education. Many of my stories are about survival and reliving them certainly didn't feel good, but it did reaffirm that there must be some faith buried deep within me in order for me to continue on despite my experiences. Confronting what I've pushed down for so long in favor of forward professional movement allowed me to take back some of my power from an institution seemingly intent on stripping it from me.

In 2013, I earned my doctorate from the University of Minnesota, one of only two Black women in my department to do so that year. In total, 2,174 doctorates were awarded in the United States to Black people that same year.[1] Of the 37 million Black people in this country, I am one of a minuscule number to reach this milestone. I secured a tenure-track job, which in this economic market is not a guarantee, and earned tenure—which is never a given. Somehow, I'm alive to tell the tale, albeit with a list of stress- and anxiety-induced ailments that have surely shortened my life span. I've made it to a position—social and intellectual, if not economic—that only faith would allow me to strive for. There were traumas along the way, to be sure, but something kept me going despite that, the same thing that keeps so many of us going despite the violence we've seen and endured: faith.

Intellectual Trauma

Black life is reduced to the experiences of trauma so often that I was reluctant to wade through the muck of my experiences for this book, but maybe that is why my intuition was calling me to end with a benediction of sorts. To examine the trauma of our ancestors means to also dredge up the remnants of ugliness and violence precipitating the trauma. The work often felt like exhuming gravesites, those of Black people I'd never know, but also of my family and my own past. Dealing with unearthed ghosts, real and imagined, both renewed those traumas and provided space to heal them. In that regard, writing this was as injurious as it was cathartic. It was institutional analysis by praxis, aggregating records of Black education and filing my own experiences among the annals of history. In much of Black culture, that understanding of our unique vulnerabilities as Black people in white supremacist environments means also believing in faith and prayer as necessary tools for protection against that negative energy we encounter daily.

The discomfort I experienced while writing only surfaced because so much of my trauma was undigested, the reluctance to revisit and deeply examine what I've been through literally stuffing me whole. This affliction weighs down entire communities of Black folks, often killing us prematurely. Active avoidance of reflection on past traumas compounds to become physical ailments, migraines, shortness of breath, sour stomach, hypertension, and constipation, many of which I personally battle. From the moment Black children recognize the difference between "us" and "them," we learn the penalties for being "us" and privileges for being "them" that can't be usurped, and we are socialized not to challenge those boundaries.

Those that do challenge these boundaries are subject to the perpetual violence of white supremacy in ways that reverberate across generations. What we haven't done much of is share our experience of trauma at school with each other—especially those of us lucky enough to be among the top 10 percent of Black earners (those who earn more than $100,000 per year; that number is more than $250,000 per year for white households),[2] we don't talk about the violence accepted in exchange for meager earnings comparative to white households.

We are complacent in our destruction by the very virtue of our continued interest in entering education despite knowing the harm we'll endure. White administrators and faculty can feign ignorance of the viciousness with which racism, sexism, and misogynoir are embedded in educational culture, but we cannot. They're quick to install us on diversity committees and other forms of race-based service on campus to maintain the illusion that Black faculty have any power to improve issues of diversity and inclusion for Black students and staff. The same universities that loudly proclaimed "Black lives matter" after the murder of George Floyd by Minneapolis police still fail to hire, retain, and promote Black faculty and students. They create Black Studies programs only to undermine them; subject Black community members to hostile, racist environments; and exploit our presence to gain public favor. These schools are not providing support and advocacy for the very folks they want to be seen as advocating for and supporting.

I didn't make it two semesters before I was nominated for and voted on to my institution's diversity committee, before I was able to even display my qualifications for the position, besides being a Black woman teaching race. I did not vote for myself, but was easily voted into the position—only to resign under duress after serving just eighteen months of a three-year term. We, the Black people who want to be here, in school, know the harm to which we're being exposed; if not, we learn quickly, and yet we remain. It is our continued presence amid active traumatization that encourages greater numbers of Black people in higher education, though with very little recognition of necessary institutional changes to improve our experiences there.

Individual persistence of Black folks in academia is not the same as institutional retention. It's often thought that because we're here—visible within the ivory tower—that it's a symbol of the administrative improvements being made at all levels of higher education. But the presence of Black students and faculty doesn't mean we feel supported or engaged by the institution. Our ability to complete degrees is often a result of grit and perseverance, non-normative access to institutional supports, or luck. In my case, it was all three, but I know a lot of Black people, women especially, who didn't make it despite the desire for higher learning and the willingness to endure violence at the hands of the academy to achieve it. I understand that a few unexpected bounces could have meant that I wouldn't be where I am today either. So instead, many of us turn to faith. We depend on individual prayers to provide the support we don't get in learning environments and hope that it's enough. Black people don't need more mentors, workshops, reading circles, or advice. We need advocates and allies with access to power and a willingness to upend power structures—even those of which they are a part, and open doors for true equality. But we rarely have these people—their very existence is a rarity.

Privileged and Powerless

I would never describe myself as an activist, but I understand my positions in higher education as inherently political; they have been every step of the way. Because I am entering spaces explicitly not for me—because my race and my gender beget imagery of violent aggressors and criminals, but not intellectuals because my class identity isn't easily described—I am an interloper in a community of legacies. I am privileged in my very access to the institution, which saps me of any external power. But I also understand that those of us on the front lines—Black professors, especially those who champion issues of race and call out racism in public view—face explicit terrorism, death threats, and threats to their careers every day.

Black faculty are expected to treat our positions as a "calling" while maintaining distance between us and the Black students we mentor, advise, and teach. Often, that means pointing out the ways in which these institutions fail Black faculty and students. Campus administrators, no matter how publicly interested in diversity and inclusion, don't want attention drawn to their failures—especially by *us*. So our research, especially on Black communities, is devalued, as is our service work as advocates for Black students on campus, while student evaluations criticizing our discussions of race in the classroom are highlighted. All of this works together to provide cover for the racially motivated tenure denials (and the heavily scrutinized approvals) we see every year.

On top of that, Black professors deal with tangible threats to our safety and belonging because we dare question institutional motivations as Black people. We may have gained access to academia, but our presence is continually unwelcome. I often imagine myself as a trespasser, an easy explanation for why life on this path feels so hard. But I realize that's what they want me to believe, want *us* to believe: that we are unfit for these environments.

We're stripped of most tangible power in learning spaces by institutional culture, and individual ideologies of white students, faculty, and administrators about who belongs in higher education, such that "professor" is a much more complicated title for me than for my white counterparts. Students, sometimes not even mine, willingly and voraciously criticize everything from my clothes to my grading policies, while fellow faculty regard me warily, gauging my political position (the assumption is always that I have one). So I walk around with this title that implies class, power, and a background that I can't actually exert, continuing on faith. Faith that I can earn a place in higher education where I will finally belong. It's the same story of the powerful ruling the powerless, the proletariat working for the bourgeoisie—the Black person living in perpetual white supremacy.

A Hope and a Prayer

My turn away from organized religion was a direct rebuke of the people I'd encountered in religious spaces rather than a distaste for religion or spirituality altogether. The hypocrisy and deception I observed taught me to distrust those trying to lead me to spiritual enlightenment, but I, like many Black folks, feel innately spiritual and the usefulness of spirit energy to guide and protect us has been repeated to me since birth. So I, not unlike the ancestors before me, repurposed my spirituality to provide a foundation of faith on which I can count when things are hard. Faith in my belonging, in support from unseen sources, in my potential for career success, in my continued health, and incoming love. My faith, this revised spirituality, is a necessary tool for surviving the overwhelming white supremacy in the majority of spaces I frequent.

Christianity, when it was introduced to the enslaved as a method of social control, also became a tool for surviving the deranged violence of slavery, a symbol of potential freedom to practicing enslaved people, repurposed as a survival mechanism in a seemingly not survivable situation. The ancestors prayed for God's protection and healing so that they may one day be free, either in the kingdom of heaven or from the literal bondage of their present realities. Religion provided faith where the potential for faith felt unlikely, hope where life was often hopeless. It's not a mistake that much of the groundwork of the civil rights movement took place among the pews and in the basements of Black churches.[3] Again and again, Black people turn to our spirituality to guide and protect us against a world seemingly intent on our demise. This book was written in the tradition of summoning faith in your own light to overcome the detriments of our identity in white worlds.

In the classroom, I've lacked power as both a student and teacher. As a student, being powerless meant exposure to unchecked violence, described as free speech discussions both at the hands of my professors and fellow peers. I was not very participatory in my first few years of college because I'd learned that speaking up meant opening myself up to even more racist comments and micro-aggressions. But I soon realized these were things I'd be subjected to whether I actively participated or not. Because my race is unchanging, so too is the likelihood of racism at HWSCUs. Silence will not protect me—but it took a lot of silence to learn that lesson.

I entered classrooms purely on hope, even as those classrooms were thick with the associated capital many Black students never access. The anxiety that I developed at school as a result physically mapped the nervousness, shortness of breath, and nausea on my neural pathways. Some days I made it through class purely on faith that I belonged even as much of what was said and done around me was specifically intended to make me feel like I did not, a contradiction reflected in my body's response. Confrontations of racism took extraordinary physical and emotional effort and an underlying belief that it would all be worth it.

In my six years as untenured faculty, I lacked the job security of many coworkers, creating a tense negotiation between career ambition and tolerance for daily racism. I still remember my first comment at a faculty meeting because of my physical nervousness in that setting. The comment popped in my mind immediately, even before the faculty member in question completed his statement, but I spent another thirty seconds negotiating with both sides of my psyche, debating the merits of speaking these thoughts aloud while also understanding that I might lose my chance if I didn't act quickly. I cursed myself for wearing a bright red sweater to work that day and took several deep breaths before finally raising my hand. As I was acknowledged (with the correct name, which is often not the case even though there are a total of ten Black women faculty on campus), I felt my hands begin to shake in anxious fear so I clasped them in front of me, and cleared my throat to shake off the sensation of its slow closing.

After the meeting adjourned and we began filing out of our meeting room, a white woman, a senior faculty member, called out to me and hurried to catch up. Identifying herself as a rare ally, she agreed with the content of my comments, but more tellingly discussed the impact regular comments like it might have on my tenure review and offered support should it be needed. That's what powerless privilege looks like. Even with a doctorate, in a room where everyone has a doctorate and is mostly white, my credentials as an untenured Black woman did not carry much weight.

Students challenging grades or course policies rarely take my word as final, and I've come to expect to meet with the dean about unhappy white students at the close of every semester. My tenure evaluation and eventual promotion hinged on the racist ideologies of the students it's my job to teach, and the faculty tasked with evaluating my work. In this way, Black faculty, especially Black women faculty, contribute more to the institution than it does to us. We are the faces of their diversity promotions, but our ideas and needs are devalued by the institution every day. Why would we continue if we didn't have faith in the potential to overcome? Hope is a currency Black people have used in exchange for survival for centuries. In some ways, the rhetoric of hope, particularly via spirituality, is the only way I know how to endure.

Rebuilding the Troops

My first Black teacher was Mr. Tinder in ninth-grade social studies. I remember him and our interactions despite their relative banality because it was my first opportunity to commune intellectually at school with a teacher who looked like me. I'd encounter a second Black teacher, a professor this time, Dr. Harriford, my sophomore year of college, and that's it. Two Black teachers over twenty-three years of education, and neither had the time nor the energy to really attend to my needs and desires as a student, at least in part because they were spread too thin, tasked with supporting a big group of students and simultaneously championing inclusion efforts within the institution.

The hardest part about a social identity where dehumanization is perpetual is not letting the constant dehumanizing experiences harden us against empathy for others, and willingness to stand on the front lines. As long as we are underrepresented in the highest ranked and most prestigious schools at every level, as staff and students, we'll continue to be subjected to white supremacist violence embedded there. It is our determination to increase our numbers in the best public high schools, at the highest ranked colleges, and as faculty and administrators that drive institutional policy as a method for improved experiences for Black people at school. When predominantly Black teachers taught Black children, the rates of graduation, college attendance, and overall academic excellence soared even under subpar circumstances. My continued presence in these spaces is built on faith that this can be an option for all Black students, again—eventually.

It is that eventuality that requires deep faith because daily micro-aggressions and experiences with racism make it easy to forget the long goal, especially when you're not sure you want to come back *tomorrow*. This is how diminished perceptions of belonging, perpetuated often by minority status in school, negatively impact the graduation and retention rates of Black students. Empirical research on the importance of belonging in school to academic achievement is readily available, but even if one doesn't want to read academic research, attending any college graduation will illustrate the continued gap between race and college achievement.

Even though Black women are increasingly attending college, the gap between white women and Black women with college degrees is as wide as it's been post-integration. We're starting college but much less likely to finish than white students. Our pictures may line the pages of university catalogs, but on campus, it's hard to conjure belonging from spaces where there's very little indication of welcomeness. I would also invite those averse to academic reading to attend one of my classes, or any class from kindergarten to graduate school, and watch the responses of Black students when they realize they have a Black teacher, watch how they engage in class discussions with more perceived support than usual.

I've heard so many Black women refer to supporting Black students as a primary reason for continuing in the face of often blatant racism while simultaneously lamenting the additional labor involved in the work of Black student support in predominantly white schools. The most painful lesson I learned in my early years on the tenure track was how taxing, and seemingly never-ending, that work would be. I spent afternoons crying in my office after listening to students unburden themselves in the safe space I provide with stories of economic, psychological, and physical distress. I've spent evenings emailing and on the phone with other Black faculty and administrators trying to strategize our best support efforts, but it's never enough. So, we continue on faith and hope that our labor makes things even incrementally better for Black students, despite the toll it takes on us.

Black women in particular are used to taking on additional labor in the community's name, regardless of our professions. My dissertation research on the career trajectories of Black women in the predominantly white cities of Minneapolis and St. Paul uncovered a conscious trade-off for time spent on engagement in local Black communities. Upward career success and time devoted to community uplift work were negatively correlated, so the more time spent in the community, the weaker their professional mobility. Those women who participated were aware of the concessions they'd made in career or community engagement, but none were regretful of their choices. The highest earners with the most professional success spent the least time volunteering in their communities. They understood the ramifications of their focus on career over community, not unlike what the former first lady Michelle Obama foresaw in her senior thesis. On the other hand, lower earners with less objectively successful careers acknowledged the impact of their community engagement on their professional success. I do not regret following my passion for learning to higher education, even as I recognize the road was filled with horrors and daily life advocating for equity on campus is exhausting.

My impacts are not just professional, they're familial as well. When my dad suggested during a catch-up call one Saturday morning last fall that I should call my cousin, Tamika, ten years older than me and often my childhood protector, I wondered what help I could offer her. "Her daughter Jada is doing so good in school, and she wants to go to college," Dad explained. "But Tamika didn't go to college. She don't know where to start. I told her to talk to you." I called, of course, and spent the next few months answering questions about applications and financial aid. Talking to both women about what to expect on college campuses, how to manage the college decision process, and economic issues to consider I found myself with secondhand excitement for this soon-to-be high school graduate—a Black woman with the world before her, not yet broken by the white supremacist world of academia.

I wish I could have that time back myself. Because that's impossible, this book is so necessary. I love that I can be a resource for my own family to traverse higher education—but I want more than that. I want to arm as many Black girls and women as I can with the knowledge about these spaces that I lacked. By laying bare my own traumas, and those of Black women before me, I am providing them the tools to protect themselves, with an understanding of how deliberately many institutions will try to undercut them.

The road to an increased Black presence on college campuses requires some Black faculty and staff to show up and challenge the racism that keeps so many others away; to make safe the spaces that for so long have been dangerous. Black students taught by Black teachers have greater academic success and mentorship, and thus our presence is an important piece of increasing Black academic success. More Black teachers mean more Black students, more Black researchers mean a greater examination of Black life, and more Black administrators mean increased dissent against white supremacist policies governing campus communities. At least, I hope so.

Activism and Prayer

I may not be an activist, but the work I do advocating for Black students on predominantly white campuses is active opposition to the preferential treatment of white members of the campus community. I didn't realize it at the time, but my perpetual entrance into prestigious and predominantly white learning spaces is activism in that it requires the white people around me to at least acknowledge the discomfort of having me in those spaces, though I cannot control whether or not they confront it. In truth, most Black faculty and students in predominantly white schools are engaged in activism. Our presence challenges who those spaces are for, and forces participants in those spaces to interact with people from whom they're generally segregated—at home, with friends, and running errands in their predominantly white neighborhoods.

White people in these spaces face forced growth or perpetual frustration. But aside from being uncomfortable, they are not traumatized by engaging in a predominantly white space where a few unexpected Black people show up. On the other hand, the experiences of Black people in predominantly white schools are traumatic. Advocating for yourself and others, searching for a mentor, and mentoring others when you're ready—that work doesn't just happen, and it's not easy. It's purposeful, stressful, and exhausting work, but it also leads to small, incremental social change important for improving the lives of Black people in academia. For other races, it may be a difficult choice, deciding to continue expecting to be traumatized in the name of progress or avoiding the trauma at the expense of others, but Black people don't usually have the same choice. We will be traumatized regardless, and throughout history, our trauma is the only thing that leads to progress.

A Black woman's success in any white supremacist space is a political statement, a middle finger to the trail of hurdled disadvantages left in her wake. The moral of this story is how incredibly ordinary it is to feel displaced as an educated Black woman. That discomfort is there by design, reinforced in the very foundation of the ivory walls, and an annoying persistence is required to bear the load on the way to success. I ended up a college professor by the grace of whichever god, force, or effort you'd attribute to accomplishing the seemingly impossible. My anger, my fear, my hunger, my barriers and blocks, and the death and life I've seen have all made me stronger. Even when I felt at my weakest and did not crumble, I certainly could have. I'm sure there are people who wish I did, yet here I am. So in this final prayer I say, keep fighting for what you want, through the extra weight, through the seeming impossibility of the thing, today and always. Have faith in your belonging, and know you're capable of success regardless of how you're treated.

My development of faith comes from understanding how unlikely my presence is in the spaces I've managed to gain access to. Looking back, as writing this book has forced me to do, I see how tenuous the relationship between luck and will has been over the course of my life. A couple of less fortuitous decisions, and a less willful personality (or equally important—a mother with a less willful personality) and I wouldn't be one of the 5 percent of PhD holders who are Black in this country. That's not to say that I've always been hyper-confident in my ability to force my way into places and professions where Black people are generally missing, but I had to develop a faith in something, the ancestors' protection, my mother's support, and especially my work ethic, to endure the continual waves of trauma at school.

The Tonic

"It used to be a tobacco plantation," my new landlord, a sixty-ish Southern white woman, said like the answer to a trivia question as we exchanged my check for her keys. She's referring to Wake Forest University in Winston-Salem, North Carolina, my first post-PhD professor position and the reason for the new digs. I returned her gaze as we concluded our business with a raised eyebrow, "Oh?" It wasn't new information, but I was surprised at how nonchalantly she mentioned this detail to a Black person, with no hint of irony, as if that was just some fun fact to pass on. I would teach on land where my ancestors were enslaved and be expected not to let that affect my experiences in the space. Despite the campus's physical beauty, it was a fact I couldn't forget, but at those times when I thought I might, the white frat bros in seersucker suits playing cro-quet and drinking beer on the quad helped remind me of the cul-ture permeating this institution.

These are the kinds of small everyday traumas pervading the lives of Black people at HWSCUs. It's also a good example of where my intellectual curiosity basically saved my life. Learning and teaching continue to be important tools for easing my traumas and doing the work to prevent similar traumas to Black students who come after me. For a long time, I attributed the things that hap-pened to me, especially at school, to personal deficiencies I needed to fix. So, I looked inward, self-inflicting additional traumas that only worsened how I felt about myself, how I felt about school, and how much faith I had in my own success. It is in the words of Black writers and researchers, and of Black students before me who'd chronicled their own experiences with racism and violence in the academy, where I discovered just how little of what I'd experienced, and will continue to experience in academic settings, was my fault.

Am I being too sensitive? Is this more than I'm capable of? Do I belong here? Those questions embedded in my consciousness and reverberating in my voice are constructed to feel and sound like they're organically mine. In reality, those messages are part of the psychological terror of education in predominantly white environments. Its primary objective is to remind us how unwelcome we are in those spaces and make us believe those feelings of non-belonging are derived internally. Faith helped me overcome and endure perpetual traumas, to believe something to be true (my impending success and upward mobility) that I can't see or touch. It's just a feeling that I should go on, a feeling that I can go on.

But that faith hasn't always been there; it took a long process of knowledge acquisition, traumatic experiences, and information synthesis. I had to go through some stuff. As I continue studying theories of construction of social groups, spaces, and order, I'm able to see the forest for the trees, understanding my place in larger racist constructs and then simultaneously lifting some of the responsibility for what's happened (and what will happen) off my own shoulders. It's a freeing feeling to remove that aspect of symbolic violence from my life, but it doesn't end the violence, or make it less traumatic. I simply have a name for it now, one that's not my own.

That's the key to closing the gap between Black and white people in the classroom, deciphering what results from racism and white supremacy rather than individual ability. This system has done an almost perfect job of perpetuating internal blame among Black people for our depressed academic achievement and then ensuring the maintenance of that depression via racist policies governing those who manage to gain access. Increased knowledge, via reading, conversation, research, and classroom experimentation, helps peel away these cultural ideologies and point out where social structures misrepresent institutional issues as individual ones. It means education can be the "salvation" for Black people Du Bois imagined, not because of the saviors in the "Talented Tenth," but because advanced learning reveals the lies of white supremacy in American education.

I recently began work with a practitioner of the Reiki energy movement. During our first meeting, she explained that all our feelings come from one of two places, love or fear; there are tangible effects on our personhood regardless of the emotional "source." The feelings derived from fear, like anxiety, anger, frustration, and disappointment can leave one feeling tired, sick, and heavy compared to feelings derived from love that make us feel energized and content. All the work I've done to fit into predominantly white learning spaces was rooted in fear of where I'd end up if I didn't perform, if I stopped playing the game.

Perhaps for me, then, ending this book with a benediction signifies not just my faith in a positive outcome, but also a request for forgiveness of my childhood self for all the shapeshifting I did, felt I had to do, to get by. Internal forgiveness for myself for all the concessions I made, micro-aggressions I didn't confront, performances I acted, and forgone emotions I never fully explored in favor of carrying on in education and continuing to pursue more. Living via a foundation of fear not only left me in poor health but also left me questioning the path I've chosen. Transitioning to a life rooted in love, love for myself with all those performances I began in childhood, love for the traumas stripped away, love for the Black and brown students benefiting from my unexpected presence in academic spaces, and maybe most importantly, love for (instead of shame about) the defense mechanisms that got me this far, but with the willingness to let those defenses go, recognizing that they no longer serve me.

This benediction then grounds the transitional process from fear to love, in faith, an internalized belief that regardless of what happens I am a whole, fully-actualized person. My reimagined faith allows me to put down so much of the weight of responsibility and worry that makes processing the structural foundations creating and intensifying negative emotions in learning spaces more difficult. Doing so helps us release and work through what we hold on to out of habit.

My story isn't everyone's story. Some Black people grew up in well-funded, diverse public schools, taught by at least a handful of Black teachers over the course of their education, and with detailed narratives about the education of their ancestors to reinforce their sense of belonging in school. Some weren't subjected to hyper-sexualization, or sexually assaulted at school. The benefits of growing up immersed in Black culture in high-quality, predominantly Black classrooms for Black children are physical, psychological, emotional, and economical. Black children in diverse schools, taught by Black teachers, are more likely to graduate high school, attend college, and complete advanced degrees. Black students with two Black teachers before third grade are 32 percent more likely to attend college. Having one Black teacher over the same time period reduces Black students' probability of dropping out of high school by 29 percent.[4]

Without those protections, I've made choices I regret to retain access to spaces where white gatekeepers were eager to keep me out. I trusted people out of necessity that didn't have my best interest at heart, and maybe most detrimental, I learned to constrict my emotional responses to feelings rooted in fear throughout my journey. That I am here and mostly whole is a claim that not all Black people who've traversed similar paths can make, and I'm grateful for that. I'm grateful for the role my spiritual faith played in my success over time, and I recognize it as foundational to my survival. But I've been in survival mode too long. Black people have been forced into perpetual survival mode for so long that sometimes it feels like our default setting. Naming the oppression I've experienced, and detailing its impact not just on my life, but on the educational experiences of entire communities of Black people, is one way to shed the generationally inherited and socially maintained need to focus on surviving rather than living.

That this is an individual choice I have to make—trying to live rather than survive in predominantly white spaces—instead of an institutional choice to address the structure and cultures of education highlights how little movement is expected to improve inclusion in educational settings. I hope that naming the structures and cultures contributing to our non-belonging at school will create an explicit public focus on the ramifications for Black students in white schools. Though everything I've experienced so far tells me not to have faith in institutional improvement, I couldn't walk into my classrooms each day, or interact cordially with my faculty coworkers, if I genuinely believed change was impossible. That would mean everything that happened to me, everything I did, was for nothing but my benefit, and given that I don't feel very "benefited," it feels like an uneven exchange. But it can't be that; there has to be recognition of the inequities of education and the impact that has on the lives of Black students, if only so our pain is not in vain. If I have faith in anything, it is in that.

Acknowledgments

I want to acknowledge my husband, Michael. I love you. Thank you for supporting my writing dreams, no matter how crazy they sound. Thanks, of course, to my mother, Robin, and sister, Jenaé, who acted as sounding boards during my writing process. I could not do life without you. To everyone who read drafts—for free, out of the kindness of your hearts, I appreciate you. And last but never least, I must acknowledge Kirsten Naito, Pedro Rodriguez, Annie Adams, and Sarah Griffin—they kept me alive at Vassar, even when they didn't realize it. I love you always.

Notes

Chapter 1

1 Winum, Jessica. "Family Ties: Vassar Legacies." *Vassar Quarterly* 97, no. 4 (2001).
2 Sullivan, Laura, Tatjana Meschede, Lars Dietrich, and Thomas Shapiro. "The Racial Wealth Gap: Why Policy Matters." Report. Institute for Assets and Social Policy, Brandeis University (2015).
3 "Black First-Year Students at the Nation's Leading Research Universities." Journal of Blacks in Higher Education Annual Survey (2013). Retrieved on May 3, 2019. https://tinyurl.com/3z7zjya8
4 "Number of Degrees Conferred by Postsecondary Institutions and Percent Change, by Race/Ethnicity and Level of Degree: Academic Years 2004–05, 2013–14, and 2014–15." National Center for Education Statistics (2015). Retrieved on May 3, 2019. https://nces.ed.gov/programs/coe/pdf/coe_svc.pdf
5 Ashenkas, Jeremy, Haeyoun Park, and Adam Pearce. "Even with Affirmative Action, Blacks and Hispanics are More Underrepresented at Top Colleges than 35 Years Ago." *New York Times* (2017) Retrieved on May 3, 2019. https://tinyurl.com/2hbssmj6
6 Ashenkas, Park, and Pearce. "Even with Affirmative Action."

7 Trostel, Philip, and Margaret Chase Smith. "It's Not Just the Money: The Benefits of College Education to Individuals and to Society." (2015). Lumina Foundation. Retrieved on May 3, 2019. https://tinyurl.com/s3w9uba8

8 "The Rising Cost of Not Going to College" (February 2014). Pew Research Center. https://tinyurl.com/4jemadhu

9 Carnevale, Anthony P., Stephen J. Rose, and Ban Cheah. "The College Payoff: Education, Occupations, Lifetime Earnings" (2011). Georgetown University Center on Education and the Workforce.

10 Patten, Eileen. "Racial, Gender Wage Gaps Persist in U.S. Despite Some Progress" (2016). Pew Research FactTank. Retrieved on May 3, 2019. https://tinyurl.com/bdy9du7x

11 Ashenkas, Park, and Pearce. "Even with Affirmative Action."

12 Sullivan, Laura, Tatjana Meschede, Lars Dietrich, and Thomas Shapiro. "The Racial Wealth Gap: Why Policy Matters" (2015). Report. Institute for Assets and Social Policy, Brandeis University.

13 Libassi, CJ. "The Neglected College Race Gap: Racial Disparities Among College Completers" (2018). Center for American Progress.

14 Jaschik, Scott. "The 2018 Surveys of Admissions Leaders: The Pressure Grows" (2018). Inside Higher Education. Retrieved on May 3, 2019. https://tinyurl.com/223uaejv

15 Jones, Janelle. "The Racial Wealth Gap: How African-Americans Have Been Shortchanged Out of the Materials to Build Wealth" (2017). Economic Policy Institute. Retrieved on May 3, 2019. https://tinyurl.com/yff3wv4h

16 Warikoo, Natasha, and Nadirah Farah Foley. "How Elite Schools Stay So White." *New York Times*, July 24, 2018. Retrieved on May 3, 2019. https://tinyurl.com/yk25pv8w

17 Warren, Earl, and Supreme Court of the United States. *U.S. Reports: Brown v. Board of Education, 347 U.S. 483.* 1953. Periodical. https://www.loc.gov/item/usrep347483/.

18 Hamilton, Darrick, and Trevor Logan. "Why Wealth Equality Remains Out of Reach for Black Americans." *The Conversation.* February 28, 2018. Retrieved on May 3, 2019. https://tinyurl.com/d6kzjzhc

19 Darity, William Jr., Darrick Hamilton, Mark Paul, Alan Aja, Anne Price, Antonio Moore, and Caterina Chiopris. 2018. "What We Get Wrong about Closing the Racial Wealth Gap." Samuel DuBois Cook Center on Social Equity, April 2018. Retrieved on May 3, 2019. https://tinyurl.com/4r4akrvc

20 Luders, Manuel, Shannon. "The Inequality Hidden Within the Race-Neutral G.I. Bill." *Jstor Daily*, September 18, 2017. Retrieved May 3, 2019. https://tinyurl.com/2p8stu95

21 Christy, R. D., and L. Williamson, eds. *A Century of Service: Land-Grant Colleges and Their Universities, 1890–1990* (New Brunswick, NJ: Transaction Publishers, 1992).

22 Christy and Williamson. *A Century of Service.*

23 Bailey, Moya, and Trudy. "On Misogynoir: Citation, Erasure, and Plagiarism." *Feminist Media Studies* 18, no. 4 (2018): 762–768.

24 Ray, Victor. "A Theory of Racialized Organizations." *American Sociological Review* 84, no. 1 (2019): 26–53.

25 Wilder, Craig Steven. *Ebony and Ivy: Race, Slavery, and the Troubled History of America's Universities.* (New York: Bloomsbury Press, 2013).

26 Flanagan, William S. and Michael E. Xie. "Median Family Income for Harvard Undergrads Triple National Average, Study Finds." *The Harvard Crimson*, January 25, 2017. Retrieved May 3, 2019. https://tinyurl.com/bdtc9e6

27 Solorzano, Daniel, and Armida Ornelas. "A Critical Race Analysis of Latina/o and African American Advanced Placement Enrollment in Public High Schools." *The High School Journal* 87, no. 3 (2004): 15–26.

28 Tyson, Karolyn. *Integration Interrupted.* (New York: Oxford Press, 2011).

29 Soares, Joseph. *SAT Wars: The Case for Test-Optional College Admissions* (New York: Teachers College Press, 2011).

30 Funderburg, Lise. "For These Families, H.B.C.U.s Aren't Just an Option. They're a Tradition." *New York Times*, May 13, 2022. Retrieved on July 22, 2022. https://tinyurl.com/4wuud447

Chapter 2

1 Ruff, Veronica. "Popular Culture: Vassar Steals the Spotlight." *Vassar Quarterly* 98, no. 2 (2002). Retrieved May 3, 2019. https://tinyurl.com/3jxvu99b

2 Diaz, Sara. "Rebecca Davis Lee Crumpler (1831–1895)." BlackPast.org. March 12, 2007. ,Retrieved May 3, 2019. https://tinyurl.com/mwu2hu4j

3 Ruff, "Popular Culture."

4 Ruff, "Popular Culture."

5 Ruff, "Popular Culture."

6 Albritton, Travis J. "Educating Our Own: The Historical Legacy of HBCUs and Their Relevance for Educating a New Generation of Leaders." *The Urban Review* 44 no. 3 (2012): 311–331.

7 Bickerstaff, Joyce. "'A Colored Girl at Vassar': The Life of Anita Florence Hemmings." *Miscellany News* 127, no.19 (1999).

8 Du Bois, W.E.B. (William Edward Burghardt). *The Souls of Black Folk; Essays and Sketches.* (Chicago, A. G. McClurg, 1903).

9 Sim, Jillian A. "Fading to White." *American Heritage* 50, no. 1 (February/March 1999). Retrieved on May 3, 2019. https://www.americanheritage.com/fading-white

10 Bates, Daisy. *The Long Shadow of Little Rock: A Memoir* (New York: David McKay, 1962).

11 The Morrill Act of 1862 (7 U.S.C. § 301)

12 The Agricultural College Act of 1890 (26 Stat. 417, 7 U.S.C. § 321)

13 Bates, *The Long Shadow*.

14 Gershenson, Seth, and Cassandra M. D. Hart, Joshua Hyman, Constance Lindsay, Nicholas W. Papageorge. "The Long-Run Impacts of Same-Race Teachers." *The National Bureau of Economic Research,* No. 25254 (2018).

15 Sabrowsky, Helen. 2019. "Examining the Lasting Legacy of the Morrill Hall Takeover." MNDaily.com.

16 Gershenson et al., "The Long-Run Impacts"

17 Gershenson et al., "The Long-Run Impacts"

18 Thomas, Claudia Lynn. "Claudia Lynn Thomas '71: Takeover of Main Building, 1969." *Vassar Encyclopedia*. Retrieved on May 3, 2019. https://tinyurl.com/422cch36

19 Bell, Derrick. *Silent Covenants: Brown v. Board of Education and the Unfulfilled Hopes for Racial Reform* (New York: Oxford University Press, 2011).

20 Bates, Daisy. *The Long Shadow of Little Rock: A Memoir*. New York: David McKay.

21 Thomas, "Takeover of Main Building, 1969."

22 Patterson, James T. *Freedom is Not Enough: The Moynihan Report and America's Struggle over Black Family Life from LBJ to Obama* (New York: Basic Books, 2010).

23 Feron, James. "Moynihan Quits Lectureship After Protest." *New York Times*, February 15, 1990. Retrieved on May 3, 2019. https://tinyurl.com/mr32vntm

24 Fultz, Michael. "African American Teachers in the South, 1890–1940: Powerlessness and the Ironies of Expectations and Protest." *History of Education Quarterly* 35, no. 4 (1995): 401–422.

25 Fultz, Michael. "Teacher Training and African American Education in the South, 1900–1940." *The Journal of Negro Education* 64, no. 2 (1995): 196–210.

26 Alterio, Maxine, and Janice McDrury. 2003. *Learning Through Storytelling in Higher Education* (London: Routledge Press, 2003).

Chapter 3

1 Geiger, A.W. "America's Public School Teachers Are Far Less Racially and Ethnically Diverse than Their Students." *Pew Research Center – Fact Tank*, 2018. Retrieved on May 3, 2019. https://tinyurl.com/324czvdx

2 US Department of Education, National Center for Education Statistics, 2018. *The Condition of Education 2018* (NCES 2018–144), Characteristics of Postsecondary Faculty.

3   Oakley, Deirdre, Jacob Stowell, and John R. Logan. "The Impact of Desegregation on Black Teachers in the Metropolis, 1970–2000." *Ethnic and Racial Studies* 39, no. 9 (2009): 1576–1598.

4   Hundley, Mary Gibson. *The Dunbar Story* (New York: Vintage Press, 1965).

5   Hundley, *The Dunbar Story.*

6   McCluskey, Audrey T. "Multiple Consciousness in the Leadership of Mary McLeod Bethune," *NWSA Journal* 6, no. 1 (1994): 69–81

7   US Department of Education, National Center for Education Statistics. (2018). *The Condition of Education 2018* (NCES 2018–144), Characteristics of Postsecondary Faculty.

8   Plessy v. Ferguson, 163 U.S. 537 (1896).

9   Spring, Joel. *The American School* (New York: John Adams, 1999).

10 Sowell, Thomas. "Dunbar High School After 100 Years." Creators.com (October 4, 2016). Retrieved on May 3, 2019. https://www.creators.com/read/thomas-sowell/10/16/dunbar-high-school-after-100-years

11 Chetty, Raj, Nathaniel Hendren, Patrick Kline, and Emmanuel Saez. "Where Is the Land of Opportunity: The Geography of Intergenerational Mobility in the United States." *Quarterly Journal of Economics* 129, no. 4 (2014): 1553–1623.

12 Chetty et al., "Where Is the Land of Opportunity"

13 Jackson, Kenneth T. *Crabgrass Frontier: The Suburbanization of the United States* (New York: Oxford University Press, 1985).

14 Gordy, Sondra. *Finding the Lost Year: What Happened When Little Rock Closed Its Public Schools?* (Little Rock, AK: University of Arkansas Press, 2008)

15 Lowe, Robert. "The Strange History of School Desegregation." *Rethinking School,* 18 no. 3 (2004).

16 Du Bois, W.E.B. (William Edward Burghardt). "Does the Negro Need Separate Schools?" *The Journal of Negro Education* 4, no. 3 (1935): 328–335.

17 Lowe, "The Strange History"

18 McGee, Ebony O., and David Stovall. "Reimagining Critical Race Theory in Education: Mental Health, Healing, and the Pathway to Liberatory Praxis." *Educational Theory,* 65 no. 5 (2015): 491–511.

19 Hauser, Christine. "Black Doctor Says Delta Flight Attendant Rejected Her; Sought 'Actual Physician.'" Newyorktimes.com, October 14, 2016. Retrieved on May 3, 2019. https://tinyurl.com/5xcyrcms

20 Gee, Michael. "Why Aren't Black Employees Getting More White-Collar Jobs?" *Harvard Business Review*, February 28, 2018. Retrieved May 3, 2019. https://tinyurl.com/2heh7pzs

21 Davis, Angela Yvonne. *Angela Davis: An Autobiography* (New York: Random House, 1974).

22 Aptheker, Bettina. *The Morning Breaks: The Trial of Angela Davis* (Ithaca: Cornell University Press, 1999).

Chapter 4

1 Coates, Ta-Nehisi. *We Were Eight Years in Power* (New York: One World Publishing, 2018).

2 Kinchen, Shirletta. "Beauty, Black Power, and Black Student Activism in Memphis." *Black Perspectives*, October 10, 2018. Retrieved May 3, 2019. https://tinyurl.com/2w94da7r

3 Velez, Mandy. "'Discriminatory': ACLU, NAACP Go After Florida School that Banned Child for Dreadlocks. TheDailyBeast.com, November 29, 2018. Retrieved May 3, 2019. https://tinyurl.com/ypftmxtv

4 Gandy, Imani. "The U.S. Supreme Court Decided to Ignore Black Hair Discrimination." Rewire.com, May 16, 2018. Retrieved on May 3, 2019. https://tinyurl.com/2428uvuj

5 Hunter, Carla D., Andrew D. Case, and I. Shevon Harvey. 2019. "Black College Students' Sense of Belonging and Racial Identity." *International Journal of Inclusive Education*, 2019.

6 Obama, Michelle. *Becoming* (New York: Crown Publishing, 2018).

7 Robinson, Michelle LaVaughn. "Princeton Educated Blacks and the Black Community." Princeton University undergraduate thesis, Department of Sociology, 1985. Retrieved on March 1, 2019. https://tinyurl.com/3m5ahhkf

8 Perkins, Linda M. "The Racial Integration of the Seven Sister Colleges." *The Journal of Blacks in Higher Education* 19 (1998): 104–108.

9 "Vassar All Torn Up," August 17, 1987. The *Providence Journal.*

10 Bly, Toi. 2017. "Mean Girls, Bring It on, and the Problem with the Unfriendly Black Hottie Narrative," 2017. Retrieved on May 3, 2019. https://www.theneuenude.com/witty/2017/4/4/bringiton

11 Pirtle, Whitney. 2019. "The Other Segregation." *The Atlantic*, April 23, 2019. Retrieved on May 3, 2019. https://tinyurl.com/yaa5xpft

12 Grissom, Jason A. 2016. "Discretion and Disproportionality: Explaining the Underrepresentation of High-Achieving Students of Color in Gifted Programs." *American Educational Research Association*, January 19, 2016. Retrieved on May 3, 2019. https://tinyurl.com/2a6dz2p6

13 Riddle, Travis, and Stacey Sinclair. "Racial Disparities in School-Based Disciplinary Actions are Associated with County-Level Rates of Racial Bias." *Proceedings of the National Academy of Sciences of the United States of America* 116 no. 17 (2019): 8255–8260.

14 Grinberg, Emmanuella. 2017. "Florida State Attorney Pulled Over in Traffic Stop that Goes Nowhere Fast." CNN.com, July 12, 2017. Retrieved on May 3, 2019. https://tinyurl.com/m35mythz

15 Goodnough, Abby. "Harvard Professor Jailed; Officer Is Accused of Bias." NewYorkTimes.com, July 21, 2009. Retrieved on May 3, 2019. https://www.nytimes.com/2009/07/21/us/21gates.html

Chapter 5

1 Hurston, Zora Neale. "How It Feels to Be a Colored Me," in *I Love Myself When I am Laughing*, New York: Feminist Press at the City University of New York (1979), 152–153.

2 Sayer, Emily. "Daisy Chain Links Commencements of Past and Present." *Miscellany News*, May 31, 2015. Retrieved on May 3, 2019. https://tinyurl.com/n8ss4nvk

3 Ballard, Allen B. *The Education of Black Folk: The Afro-American Struggle for Knowledge in White America* (New York: Harper & Row, 1973).

4 Otterman, Sharon. "Black Columbia Student's Confrontation With Security Becomes Flashpoint Over Racism on Campus." NewYorkTimes.com, April 18, 2019. https://tinyurl.com/yp32md68

5 Goffman, Erving. *The Presentation of Self in Everyday Life* (New York: Doubleday, 1959).

6 Harris-LaMothe, Jasmine. "The Negotiators: Black Professional Women, Success, and the Management of Competing Identities," 2013. Retrieved from the University of Minnesota Digital Conservancy.

7 Goffman, Erving. *The Presentation of Self in Everyday Life* (New York: Doubleday, 1959).

8 Cornelius, Janet. "'We Slipped and Learned to Read': Slave Accounts of the Literacy Process, 1830–1865." *Phylon (1960-)* 44 no. 3 (1983): 171–186.

9 Mills, Charles W. *The Racial Contract* (Ithaca: Cornell University Press: 1997).

10 Bauer-Wolf, Jeremy. "Hate Incidents on Campus Still Rising." InsideHigherEducation.com, February 25, 2019. Retrieved on May 3, 2019. https://tinyurl.com/4knzck4z

11 Axford, William. "Fox Anchors Call Houston Teen Accepted to 20 Colleges 'Obnoxious.'" *Houston Chronicle*, April 10, 2018. Retrieved on May 3, 2019. https://tinyurl.com/2uf48eb9

12 Wright, Earl II. *The First American School of Sociology: W. E. B. Du Bois and the Atlanta Sociological Laboratory* (New York: Routledge, 2016).

13 Pearson, Willie. *Black Scientists, White Society, and Colorless Science: A Study of Universalism in American Science* (Millwood, NY: Gateway/Associated Faculty Press, 1985).

14 Simba, Malik. 2007. "E. Franklin Frazier (1894–1962)." Blackpast.org, January 19, 2007. Retrieved on May 3, 2019. https://tinyurl.com/zsbynf2p

Chapter 6

1 Geronimus A.T., M.T. Hicken, J.A. Pearson, S.J. Seashots, K.L. Brown and T.D. Cruz. "Do U.S. Black Women Experience Stress-Related

Accelerated Biological Aging? A Novel Theory and First Population-Based Test of Black-White Differences in Telomere Length." *Hum Nat* 21 (2010): 19–38.

2 Blad, Evie, and Alex Harwin. "Black Students More Likely to Be Arrested at School." *Education Week*, January 25, 2017. Retrieved on May 3, 2019. https://tinyurl.com/mr39a7nn

3 Scully, Pamela, and Clifton Crais "Race and Erasure: Sara Baartman and Hendrik Cesars in Cape Town and London." *Journal of British Studies* 47 no. 2 (2008): 301–323.

4 2018 Student Experiences Survey. Duke University, Retrieved on May 3, 2019. https://students.duke.edu/wp-content/uploads/2022/11/Student-Experience-Survey_02.18.19.pdf

5 Haidarali, Laila. *Brown Beauty* (New York: NYU Press, 2017).

6 Young, Andrew. "AEPi Fraternity to be Removed from Temple's Campus." TempleUpdate.com, November 30, 2018. Retrieved on May 3, 2019. https://tinyurl.com/bdh6rjhj

7 Mack, Justin L. "Indiana University Chapter of Kappa Sigma Fraternity Pulled by National Headquarters." *Indianapolis Star*, December 5, 2018. Retrieved on May 3, 2019. https://tinyurl.com/2p8ryvu8

8 Corey, Dan. "University of Michigan Fraternity Council Cancels All Greek Life Activities." NBCNews.com, November 10, 2017. Retrieved on May 3, 2019. https://tinyurl.com/23bsvpjr

9 Rocheleau, Matt. "Dartmouth Bans Hard Alcohol, Forbids Greek Life Pledging." *Boston Globe, January 29, 2015.* Retrieved on May 3, 2019. https://tinyurl.com/2p93j8d8

10 Cantor, David, Bonnie Fisher, Susan Chibnall, and Reanna Townsend. "Report on the AAU Campus Climate Survey on Sexual Assault and Sexual Misconduct." *Westat*, September 21, 2015. Retrieved on May 3, 2019. https://tinyurl.com/mry7ra3u

11 Cooper, Jayne, Elizabeth Murphy, Roger Webb, Keith Hawton, Helen Bergen, Keith Waters, and Navneet Kapur. "Ethnic Differences in Self-Harm, Rates, Characteristics and Service Provision: Three-City Cohort Study." *British Journal of Psychiatry* 197, no. 3 (2010): 212–218.

Chapter 7

1 "History of Apple Valley High School." Apple Valley High School. Independent School District No. 196. Retrieved on May 6, 2007.

2 Callis, Robert R., and Melissa Kresin "Residential Vacancies and Homeownership in the Fourth Quarter 2014," 2015. Retrieved May 3, 2018. http://www.census.gov/housing/hvs/files/currenthvspress.pdf

3 Ray, Rashawn. "Black People Don't Exercise in My Neighborhood: Perceptions of the Built Environment on the Physical Activity of Middle-Class Blacks and Whites." *Social Science Research* 66 (2017): 42–57.

4 Carpenter, James. "Thomas Jefferson and the Ideology of Democratic Schooling." *Democracy & Education* 21, no. 2 (2013): 1–11.

5 "Brown v. Board: Timeline of School Integration in the US." April 2004.

6 Bly, Antonio T. "Slave Literacy and Education in Virginia." EncyclopediaVirginia.com Retrieved on May 3, 2019. https://tinyurl.com/4kenun8s

7 Groen, Mark. "The Whig Party and the Rise of Common Schools, 1837–1854." *American Educational History Journal* 35, no. 1/2 (2008): 251–260.

8 Ewalt, David M. "America's Best Prep Schools." Forbes.com, April 29, 2010. Retrieved on May 3, 2019. https://tinyurl.com/35mecznk

9 Jackson, Kenneth T. *Crabgrass Frontier: The Suburbanization of the United States* (New York: Oxford University Press, 1985).

10 Heller, Donald E. "Pell Grant Recipients in Selective Colleges and Universities." *The Century Foundation.* Retrieved on May 3, 2019. https://tinyurl.com/2h4hyf3m

11 Meece, Melissa. "2001–2002 Tuition Fees Increase." *Miscellany News.* April 6, 2001. Retrieved on May 3, 2019. https://tinyurl.com/43jy3vam

12 Berman, Jillian, and Jay Zehngebot. "Paying for Your College, 30 Years Ago vs. Today." MarketWatch.com, 2017. Retrieved May 3, 2019. https://www.marketwatch.com/graphics/college-debt-now-and-then/

13 McDonald, Judith A., and Robert J. Thornton. "Do New Male and Female College Graduates Receive Unequal Pay?" *The Journal of Human Resources* 42, no. 1 (2007): 32–48.

14 Van Dam, Andrew. "People from Elite Backgrounds Increasingly Dominate Academia, Data Shows," *Washington Post*, July 8, 2022. Retrieved on July 22, 2022. https://tinyurl.com/yvxskh7c

15 Huelsman, Mark. "The Debt Divide: The Racial and Class Bias Behind the "New Normal" of Student Borrowing." *Demos*, May 19, 2015. Retrieved on May 3, 2019. https://tinyurl.com/2ruj8vj2

16 Meschede, Tatjana, and Joanna Taylor. "Inherited Prospects: The Importance of Financial Transfers for White and Black College–Educated Households' Wealth Trajectories" 77, no. 3/4 (2018): 1048–1076.

17 Hannon, Kerry. "At Vassar a Focus on Diversity and Affordability in Higher Education," *New York Times*, June 23, 2016. Retrieved on May 3, 2019. https://tinyurl.com/5fad7pvb

18 Downs, Kenya. "Why is Milwaukee so Bad for Black People?" *PBS News Hour*, February 8, 2016. Retrieved on May 3, 2019. https://tinyurl.com/ytsmzyxa

19 hooks, bell. *Where We Stand: Class Matter* (New York: Routledge, 2000).

20 Dettling, Lisa J., Joanne W. Hsu, Lindsay Jacobs, Kevin B. Moore, and Jeffrey P. Thompson. "Recent Trends in Wealth-Holding by Race and Ethnicity: Evidence from the Survey of Consumer Finances." FEDS Notes September 27, 2017, Board of Governors of the Federal Reserve System (US).

21 Johnson, Nate. "College Costs, Prices and the Great Recession." The Lumina Foundation, 2014.

22 Seamster, Louise. "Black Debt, White Debt." *Contexts*, 18, no. 1 (2019): 30–35.

23 Osoro, Sam, Tatjana Meschede, and Thomas Shapiro. "The Roots of the Widening Racial Wealth Gap: Explaining the Black-White Economic Divide." Institute on Assets & Social Policy at Brandeis University, 2013. Retrieved on May 3, 2019. https://tinyurl.com/ytccu3bh

24 White, Gillian B. "The Recession's Racial Slant." *The Atlantic*, June 24, 2015. Retrieved May 3, 2019. https://tinyurl.com/48s9exfd

Chapter 8

1 NSF, NIH, USED, USDA, NEH, NASA, Survey of Earned Doctorates 2004–2014. "TABLE 19. Doctorate Recipients, by Ethnicity, Race, and Citizenship Status: 2004–14." Retrieved on May 3, 2019. https://www.nsf.gov/statistics/2016/nsf16300/data/tab19.pdf

2 Fontenot, Kayla, Jessica Semega, and Melissa Kollar. "Current Population Reports, P60–263, Income and Poverty in the United States: 2017" *US Census Bureau*, 2018.

3 Calhoun-Brown, Allison. "Upon This Rock: The Black Church, Nonviolence, and the Civil Rights Movement." *Politic Science and Politics* 33, no. 2 (2000): 168–174.

4 Gershenson, Seth, Cassandra Hart, Joshua Hyman, Constance Lindsay, and Nicholas W. Papageorge. 2018. "The Long-Run Impacts of Same-Race Teachers." NBER Working Paper No. w25254.